Better Homes and Gardens®

ORIENTAL RECIPES

BETTER HOMES AND GARDENS® BOOKS

Editor Gerald M. Knox
Art Director Ernest Shelton
Managing Editor David A. Kirchner
Editorial Project Managers James D. Blume, Marsha Jahns, Rosanne Weber Mattson, Mary Helen Schiltz

Food and Nutrition Editor Nancy Byal
Department Head, Cook Books Sharyl Heiken
Associate Department Heads Sandra Granseth, Rosemary C. Hutchinson, Elizabeth Woolever
Senior Food Editors Julia Malloy, Marcia Stanley, Joyce Trollope
Associate Food Editors Linda Henry, Mary Major, Diana McMillen, Mary Jo Plutt, Maureen Powers, Martha Schiel, Linda Foley Woodrum
Recipe Development Editor Marion Viall
Test Kitchen Director Sharon Stilwell
Test Kitchen Photo Studio Director Janet Pittman
Test Kitchen Home Economists Lynn Blanchard, Jean Brekke, Kay Cargill, Marilyn Cornelius, Jennifer Darling, Maryellyn Krantz, Lynelle Munn, Dianna Nolin, Marge Steenson

Associate Art Directors Linda Ford Vermie, Neoma Alt West, Randall Yontz
Assistant Art Directors Lynda Haupert, Harijs Priekulis, Tom Wegner
Senior Graphic Designer Darla Whipple-Frain
Graphic Designers Mike Burns, Brian Wignall

Vice President, Editorial Director Doris Eby
Executive Director, Editorial Services Duane L. Gregg

President, Book Group Fred Stines
Director of Publishing Robert B. Nelson
Vice President, Retail Marketing Jamie Martin
Vice President, Direct Marketing Arthur Heydendael

Oriental Recipes
Contributing Editor Lorene Frohling
Copy and Production Editor Marsha Jahns
Graphic Designer Lynda Haupert
Electronic Text Processor Donna Russell
Photographers Michael Jensen and Sean Fitzgerald
Food Stylists Suzanne Finley, Dianna Nolin, Janet Pittman, Maria Rolandelli

On the cover
Beef and Peppers in Black Bean Sauce (see recipe, page 30)

Our seal assures you that every recipe in *Oriental Recipes* has been tested in the Better Homes and Gardens® Test Kitchen. This means that each recipe is practical and reliable, and meets our high standards of taste appeal.

Oriental cooking—delicious, exciting, intriguing—is as much fun to create as it is to eat. It's a delightful food adventure filled with age-old cooking techniques and wonderful taste sensations.

Begin your culinary journey by browsing through *Oriental Recipes* for a sampling of the many specialties you've enjoyed in Oriental restaurants. Then, venture beyond the familiar to the extraordinary—sizzling satés, delicate steamed buns, delectable dim sum, and much, much more.

No need to worry about trying unfamiliar recipes, because we give you lots of help. We've fashioned the know-how of Oriental cooks into simple-to-follow directions throughout each chapter.

Puzzled by an unusual ingredient? Check our handy ingredient guide before you head for the market. Or, if you prefer to use a more common ingredient, try our practical suggestions for substitutes.

Contents

Introduction
3

Oriental Roasting
6

Lively marinades lend flavor and pizzazz to roasted pork and poultry.

Red-Cooking
12

Red-cooking gently simmers poultry or meat in a spicy soy sauce stock.

Pan-Fried Noodles
42

Shaped into a noodle cake and browned, egg noodles are delicious topped with a savory stir-fry.

Bubbling Hot Pots
48

Follow the Oriental custom of cooking at the table. It's fun for everyone.

Delectable Egg Dumplings
54

Tempting, mouth-watering dumplings–perfect for a special brunch, lunch, or supper dish.

Sensational Sushi
58

Try your hand at making homemade sushi, the Japanese snacks sculpted from rice and seafood.

Versatile Wontons
86

Simmering or deep-frying— *you* choose the method to cook these flavor-packed morsels.

Crispy Spring Rolls
90

Rice papers make an impressive wrap for tasty Vietnamese snacks.

Progressive Dim Sum Party
94

A novel party idea for Oriental-food buffs.

Szechwan Duck
102

Steaming and deep-frying combine to create a delectable Oriental masterpiece.

Savory Soups
16

Relish the aroma and flavor of Oriental soups, a mealtime staple in Far Eastern countries.

Stir-Fry Cooking
22

Learn the fun and excitement of stir-frying, using vegetables and Oriental seasonings.

House Specialties From the Wok
28

A sampling of our favorite stir-fry entrées from Oriental restaurants.

Stir-Fried Rice
36

A creative stir-fry using leftovers, fried rice is served in many versions throughout the Orient.

Over the Fire
62

Sizzling satés and seafood capture the spirit and flavor of Oriental cooking in an outdoor setting.

Steam Cooking
68

Expand your steaming know-how by including a variety of foods, from main dishes to desserts.

Silver-Thread Buns
76

Unique in design, these marvelous steamed buns are showstoppers at any special dinner party.

Deep-Fried Favorites
80

Make these deep-fried Oriental dishes a specialty at your house.

Oriental Dinner Party
106

Share your culinary expertise with friends at a dinner with an Oriental flair.

Oriental Ingredients
114

Special Helps
Turn to this ingredient guide when questions arise.

Nutrition Analysis Chart
122

Index
125

Oriental Roasting

Tender and succulent—
that's Oriental roasting at
its best. Now the centuries-
old secret of Oriental
roasting is yours with our
simple marinades.
Tantalizingly spiced, these
marinades transform pork
and poultry into delectable
dishes you'll desire often.

   Turn the page, and
discover the captivating
taste of the Orient.

Oven-Roasted Spareribs

Oven-Roasted Spareribs

Buying Oriental ingredients in your supermarket is often easier than you think. But if you're unfamiliar with an ingredient, check the Special Helps (see pages 114–121) before you shop

⅓ **cup soy sauce**
2 **tablespoons rice wine *or* dry sherry**
2 **tablespoons hoisin sauce**
1 **tablespoon cooking oil**
1 **teaspoon five-spice powder *or* Five-Spice Powder (see tip, page 11)**
1 **clove garlic, minced***
¼ **teaspoon pepper**
2 **pounds pork loin back ribs *or* meaty spareribs, sawed in half across bones**
½ **cup bottled plum sauce *or* Plum Sauce (see tip, page 11)**
   Cucumber Sticks (optional) (see tip, opposite)
   Fresh cilantro *or* parsley (optional)

For marinade, in a small mixing bowl combine soy sauce, rice wine or dry sherry, hoisin sauce, oil, five-spice powder, garlic, and pepper.

Cut meat into single-rib portions. Trim separable fat from ribs. Place ribs in a plastic bag. Set the bag in a deep bowl. Pour marinade over ribs (see photo 1). Close the bag tightly and turn to coat ribs. Marinate in the refrigerator for 4 hours or overnight; turn the bag occasionally.

Line the bottom of a broiler pan with foil. Top with a broiler rack. Remove ribs from the bag and place, meaty side down, on the unheated rack (see photo 2). Set marinade aside. Roast ribs in a 375° oven for 40 minutes or till no pink remains, turning and brushing twice with reserved marinade (see photo 3).

Brush with plum sauce. Turn ribs and brush again. Roast for 5 minutes more. To serve, arrange ribs on a serving platter. If desired, garnish with Cucumber Sticks and cilantro or parsley. Makes about 20 appetizer servings.

**See cutting technique, page 27.*

1 Pour the marinade over the meat in a plastic bag that's set in a deep bowl. The bowl makes moving the bag easier and reduces cleanup chores should the bag leak.

2 Transfer the meat from the plastic bag to the broiler rack, letting the excess marinade drip back into the bag.

3 Brush the meat with the reserved marinade, using a basting brush. Basting keeps the meat moist as it roasts, and adds flavor, too.

Cucumber Sticks: Select a medium-size cucumber that has few or small seeds, such as Burpless, English, or seedless cucumber. Bias-slice the cucumber into ¼-inch-thick slices, discarding the ends. Stack 3 or 4 slices together, then cut the stack into ¼-inch-thick sticks, as shown. Stack and cut the remaining cucumber slices into sticks.

Chinese Roast Pork

Serve this Cantonese-style roast pork as a tasty appetizer. Add leftovers to fried rice (see recipe, page 38).

¼ **cup hoisin sauce**
¼ **cup soy sauce**
2 **tablespoons dry sherry**
2 **tablespoons honey**
1 **teaspoon grated gingerroot***
1 **small clove garlic, minced***
½ **teaspoon five-spice powder *or***
    Five-Spice Powder (see tip, opposite)
1 **3-pound pork sirloin roast**
    Hot Mustard Sauce, bottled plum
    sauce, *or* Plum Sauce (see tip,
    opposite) (optional)
    Toasted Sesame Seed (optional)

For marinade, in a small mixing bowl combine hoisin sauce, soy sauce, dry sherry, honey, gingerroot, garlic, and five-spice powder; set aside.

Trim bone and separable fat from pork. Cut pork crosswise into 1-inch-thick slices. Place pork slices in a plastic bag. Set the bag in a deep bowl. Pour marinade over pork (see photo 1, page 8). Close the bag tightly and turn to coat pork. Marinate in the refrigerator for 6 hours or overnight, turning the bag occasionally. Meanwhile, prepare Hot Mustard Sauce or Plum Sauce and Toasted Sesame Seed, if desired.

Line the bottom of a broiler pan with foil. Top with a broiler rack. Remove pork from the bag and place on the unheated rack (see photo 2, page 8). Set marinade aside. Roast pork in a 350° oven for 30 to 35 minutes or till no pink remains, turning and brushing occasionally with reserved marinade (see photo 3, page 9).

Cut pork into thin strips; sprinkle with Toasted Sesame Seed, if desired. Serve with sauce for dipping, if desired. Makes about 16 appetizer servings or 1¼ pounds meat.

Hot Mustard Sauce: In a small mixing bowl combine ¼ cup *dry mustard* and 1 teaspoon *sesame oil* or *cooking oil*. (Or, for a spicier sauce, substitute ½ teaspoon *chili oil or Chili Oil* [see tip, opposite] for sesame oil *or* cooking oil.) Gradually stir in 3 tablespoons *water*. Serve at room temperature. Makes about ¼ cup.

Toasted Sesame Seed: Spread *sesame seed* in a thin layer in a shallow baking pan. Bake in a 350° oven for 7 to 10 minutes or till light brown, stirring once or twice.

Chicken in Soy Sauce

An Indonesian dish spiced with a sweet soy marinade.

1 **large onion, finely chopped (1 cup)**
2 **cloves garlic, minced***
1 **tablespoon Oriental chili paste**
2 **tablespoons cooking oil**
⅓ **cup lemon juice**
¼ **cup sweet soy sauce *or* Sweet Soy Sauce**
    (see tip, opposite)
1 **2½- to 3-pound broiler-fryer chicken,**
    cut up

For marinade, in a medium skillet cook onion, garlic, and chili paste in hot oil till onion is tender but not brown. Remove from heat; stir in lemon juice and sweet soy sauce. Cool.

Meanwhile, rinse chicken, then pat dry. Place chicken in a plastic bag. Set the bag in a deep bowl. Pour marinade over chicken (see photo 1, page 8). Close the bag tightly and turn to coat chicken. Marinate in the refrigerator for 4 hours or overnight, turning the bag occasionally.

Line the bottom of a broiler pan with foil. Top with a lightly greased broiler rack. Remove chicken from the bag and place on the unheated rack (see photo 2, page 8). Set marinade aside. Roast chicken in a 375° oven for 40 to 45 minutes or till tender, turning and brushing occasionally with reserved marinade (see photo 3, page 9). Transfer to a serving platter; garnish with lemon twists, if desired. Serves 6.

*See cutting technique, page 27.

Homemade Ingredients

Sometimes Oriental cooking and unfamiliar ingredients seem to go hand in hand. To avoid searching for some of these unusual ingredients, use our easy-to-make homemade recipes as substitutes for similar commercial products. These recipes make use of readily available ingredients and take little time to prepare in your kitchen.

Sesame Paste
In a food processor bowl or blender container place ⅔ cup *sesame seed*. Cover and process or blend to a fine powder. Through the hole in the lid or with the lid ajar, gradually add 2 tablespoons *cooking oil,* processing or blending till mixture is smooth. Cover and store in the refrigerator. Makes ⅓ cup.

Plum Sauce
In a small saucepan combine one 12-ounce jar *plum preserves;* 2 tablespoons *vinegar;* 1 tablespoon *brown sugar;* 1 tablespoon finely chopped *onion;* 1 teaspoon seeded and finely chopped dried *red chili pepper* (see tip Note, page 30) *or* 1 teaspoon crushed *red pepper;* 1 clove *garlic,* minced;* and ½ teaspoon ground *ginger*. Bring to boiling, stirring constantly. Remove from heat; cover and chill overnight. Makes 1¼ cups.

Chili Oil
In a small saucepan heat ⅓ cup *cooking oil*** and 2 tablespoons *sesame oil* to 365°. Remove from heat. Stir in 2 teaspoons ground *red pepper*. Cool. Strain. Cover and store in the refrigerator. Makes about ½ cup.
***Note:** For milder flavor, increase *cooking oil* to ½ cup.

Sweet Soy Sauce
In a heavy 10-inch skillet heat 1½ cups *sugar* over medium heat till it begins to melt, without stirring. Once the sugar begins to melt, cook and stir for 2 to 3 minutes or till golden. Remove from heat.

Slowly and carefully stir in ¾ cup *water;* ¾ cup *soy sauce;* and 1 *star anise,* finely crushed, *or* 1 teaspoon *aniseed*. (Watch for spattering.) Return the skillet to the heat. Bring to boiling; reduce heat. Simmer about 15 minutes or till mixture is slightly thickened and sugar is dissolved, stirring constantly. Cool to room temperature.

Skim off foam and any anise that floats to the top. Strain to remove additional anise. Cover and store in the refrigerator. Makes about 1⅓ cups.

Dried Tangerine Peel
Using a vegetable peeler, thinly slice peel from 3 *tangerines or oranges* into 1½x½-inch strips; scrape off excess white membrane. Place tangerine or orange strips in a single layer on a baking sheet.

Bake in a 300° oven till strips are dried. Allow 7 to 10 minutes for tangerine peel and 10 to 12 minutes for orange peel. Store dried peel in a covered container. Makes ⅓ cup.

Five-Spice Powder
In a small mixing bowl combine 1 teaspoon ground *cinnamon;* 1 *star anise,* finely crushed, *or* 1 teaspoon *aniseed;* ¼ teaspoon *fennel seed,* crushed; ¼ teaspoon whole *Szechwan peppers or* whole *black peppers,* crushed; and ⅛ teaspoon ground *cloves*. Store mixture in a covered container. Makes 2 teaspoons.

Red-Cooking

Often overlooked and underrated, red-cooking deserves equal billing with stir-frying as truly authentic Chinese cooking.

Red-cooking simmers food in a spicy soy sauce stock, imparting a rich, robust flavor. As the name suggests, the well-seasoned stock also adds a very handsome reddish-brown color to the food.

Give this Chinese specialty center stage at mealtime, and enjoy the applause.

Red-Cooked Chicken

Red-Cooked Chicken

3 tablespoons dried tangerine peel
  or Dried Tangerine Peel (see tip,
  page 11)
1 tablespoon whole Szechwan peppers
  or whole black peppers
3 inches stick cinnamon
1 star anise or 1 teaspoon aniseed
3 cups water
1 cup soy sauce
½ cup rice wine or dry sherry
4 green onions, cut into 1-inch pieces
3 tablespoons brown sugar
1 2½- to 3-pound broiler-fryer chicken
  Carrot Flowers (optional)
    (see tip, right)
  Green onion slivers* (optional)

For spice bag, wrap tangerine peel, Szechwan or black peppers, cinnamon, and star anise or aniseed in cheesecloth (see photo 1). In a 4- or 5-quart Dutch oven mix water, soy sauce, rice wine or dry sherry, green onion pieces, brown sugar, and spice bag. Bring to boiling.

Rinse chicken. Place in soy sauce mixture, breast side down. Spoon soy sauce mixture over chicken (see photo 2). Return to boiling; reduce heat. Cover and simmer for 25 minutes.

Turn chicken. Baste again with cooking liquid. Simmer, covered, for 25 to 30 minutes more or till chicken is tender, basting often with cooking liquid during the last 10 minutes.

Transfer chicken to a serving platter; reserve cooking liquid. If desired, garnish chicken with Carrot Flowers and green onion slivers. Strain reserved liquid (see photo 3). Skim fat from liquid. Store liquid in the refrigerator for up to 3 days or in the freezer for up to 6 months. Reuse for other red-cooked dishes. Makes 6 servings.

Red-Cooked Squabs or Cornish Game Hens: Prepare Red-Cooked Chicken as above, *except* substitute four 12- to 14-ounce *squabs or* two 1- to 1½-pound *Cornish game hens* for chicken. Reduce the first cooking time to 20

* *See cutting technique, page 27.*

minutes. Turn and baste (see photo 2). Simmer, covered, till tender, basting often during the last 10 minutes. Allow 15 to 20 minutes for squabs and 20 to 25 minutes for hens. Serve squabs whole or halve hens lengthwise. If desired, garnish as above. Makes 4 servings.

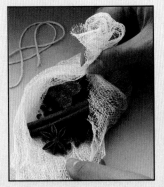

1 Place the spices on a double layer of cheesecloth. Gather the cloth edges together over the spices, as shown. Tie with string.

2 Using a large spoon, baste the food with the soy sauce mixture. Basting adds flavor, color, and moisture to the surface of the food.

Carrot Flowers: Cut 1 large carrot into 2- to 3-inch lengths. For each section, make a ¼-inch-deep lengthwise cut. Cut again at an angle to the first cut to form a V-shaped wedge; remove the wedge. Cut 3 more wedges around the carrot. Cut the carrot sections into ⅛- to ¼-inch-thick slices.

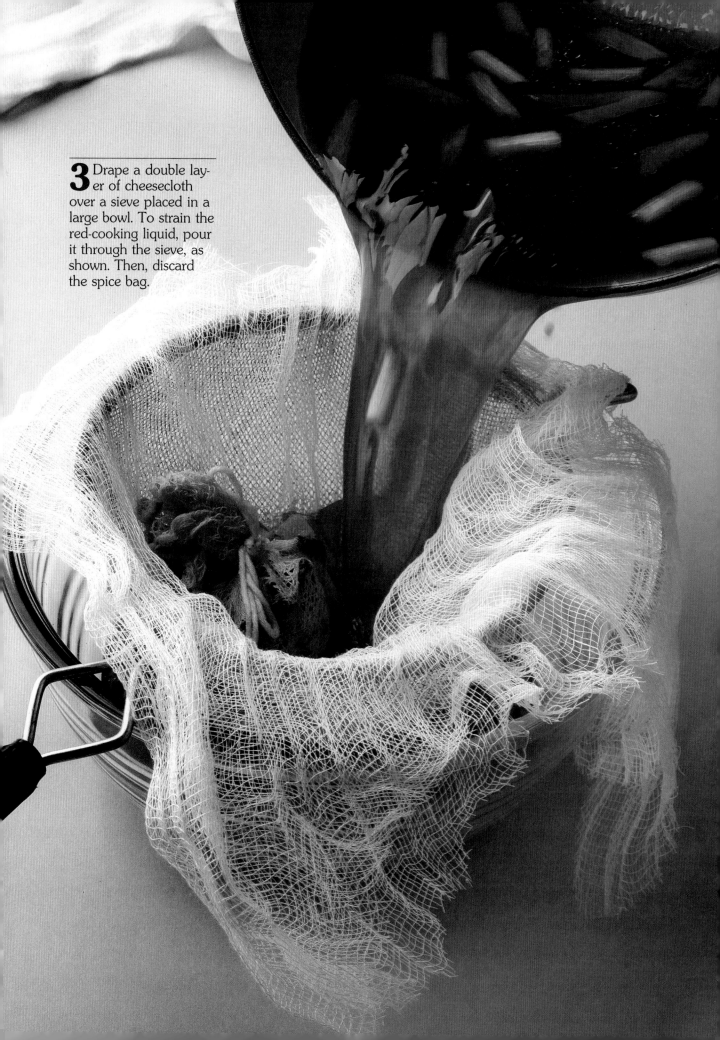

3 Drape a double layer of cheesecloth over a sieve placed in a large bowl. To strain the red-cooking liquid, pour it through the sieve, as shown. Then, discard the spice bag.

Savory Soups

Hot soup is as much a mealtime staple as the ever-present rice bowl in the Orient. Traditionally, the soup is brought to the table in a communal pot, and all those around the table serve themselves throughout the meal.

Refreshing Far Eastern soups both quench the diners' thirsts, and offer a savory flavor to the meal.

Spicy Chicken Soup

Spicy Chicken Soup

Made with rice sticks, this Southeast Asian soup is seasoned with a spice blend reminiscent of curry. If you don't have rice sticks, use cooked spaghetti or fine egg noodles as a substitute.

1   **ounce rice sticks**
     Fried Onion Flakes (see tip, opposite)
1   **whole medium chicken breast**
         (about 12 ounces), skinned and boned
         (see tip, page 34)
½   **teaspoon ground coriander**
½   **teaspoon shrimp paste *or* anchovy paste**
¼   **teaspoon ground turmeric**
¼   **teaspoon ground cumin**
2   **tablespoons water**
1   **medium onion, chopped (½ cup)**
2   **tablespoons finely chopped**
         macadamia nuts *or* blanched almonds
1   **clove garlic, minced***
1   **teaspoon grated gingerroot***
1   **tablespoon cooking oil**
4   **cups chicken broth**
2   **teaspoons lemon juice**
1   **medium potato, peeled, cooked, and**
         chopped
1   **hard-cooked egg, coarsely chopped**
2   **green onions, thinly sliced**

In a medium mixing bowl soak rice sticks in enough hot water to cover for 30 minutes. Drain well. Cut rice sticks into 3-inch lengths (see photo 1). Set aside. Prepare Fried Onion Flakes. Cut chicken into bite-size pieces.

In a small mixing bowl combine coriander, shrimp paste or anchovy paste, turmeric, and cumin; gradually stir in water. In a large saucepan cook chopped onion, macadamia nuts or almonds, garlic, and gingerroot in hot oil over medium-high heat for 3 to 4 minutes or till onion is tender but not brown, stirring often-

.Add coriander mixture; cook and stir for 1 minute. Add broth and chicken; bring to boiling. Reduce heat; cover and simmer for 5 minutes (see photo 2).

Add rice sticks. Cook, uncovered, for 5 minutes, stirring occasionally. Add lemon juice. Divide potato, hard-cooked egg, and green onions among 4 soup bowls. Top with broth mixture (see photo 3). Sprinkle with *2 to 3 teaspoons* of the Fried Onion Flakes. Makes 4 servings.

1 After soaking and draining the rice sticks, cut them into 3-inch lengths, using a sharp knife. Use the same technique for cutting bean threads.

* *See cutting technique, page 27.*

Fried Onion Flakes:
Stir ½ cup dried minced *onion* in 1 tablespoon hot *cooking oil* over medium heat for 3 to 4 minutes or till golden brown. Drain on paper towels. Cool. Store in the refrigerator. Sprinkle over soups and salads. Makes ½ cup.

2 As the broth mixture begins to boil, reduce the heat to simmer, and cover the saucepan. Gentle simmering enhances the flavor of the soup.

3 Ladle the soup from the saucepan into individual soup bowls and serve immediately. Unlike most soups, Spicy Chicken Soup is served *over* the garnishes, as shown.

Hot and Sour Shrimp Soup

A Thai soup punctuated with hot chilies and a tangy citrus flavor.

12 ounces fresh *or* frozen medium shrimp in shells
2 stalks lemongrass
1 tablespoon cooking oil
4 cups chicken broth
  Lemon peel (about 2x1-inch rectangle), cut into strips
  Lime peel (about 1-inch square), cut into strips
1 green serrano *or* jalapeño pepper, seeded and chopped (see tip Note, page 30)
1 green onion, thinly sliced
1 tablespoon lime juice
2 teaspoons fish sauce
  Snipped fresh cilantro *or* parsley
1 red *or* green serrano pepper, seeded and finely chopped (optional)

Thaw shrimp, if frozen; rinse. Peel and devein, reserving shells (see tip, opposite). Halve shrimp lengthwise; set aside. Discard outer layers of lemongrass; cut stalks into 1-inch pieces.

In a large saucepan cook reserved shrimp shells in hot oil over medium-high heat till shells turn pink, stirring often. Add lemongrass, chicken broth, lemon peel, lime peel, and 1 serrano or jalapeño pepper. Bring mixture to boiling. Reduce heat; cover and simmer for 20 minutes (see photo 2, page 19).

Strain broth through a sieve lined with cheesecloth (see photo 3, page 15). Return broth to saucepan; bring to boiling. Add shrimp. Return to boiling; reduce heat and simmer, uncovered, for 1 to 2 minutes or till shrimp turn pink, stirring occasionally.

Stir in green onion, lime juice, and fish sauce; heat for 1 minute. Ladle into soup bowls (see photo 3, page 19). Garnish with cilantro or parsley and red or green serrano pepper, if desired. Makes 4 servings.

*See cutting technique, page 27.

Korean Beef Soup

6 ounces cooked beef
1 medium onion, chopped (½ cup)
1 tablespoon sesame oil *or* cooking oil
2 cloves garlic, minced*
1 teaspoon grated gingerroot*
1 to 2 teaspoons Korean chili sauce *or* hot bean paste, *or* ½ teaspoon ground red pepper
4 cups beef broth
1 cup fresh bean sprouts
1 medium carrot, cut into julienne strips*
  Green onion slivers*

Cut beef into matchstick-size shreds (see tip, page 35). (You should have 1¼ cups.) In a large saucepan cook onion in hot sesame oil or cooking oil over medium-high heat for 2 minutes, stirring often.

Stir in garlic; gingerroot; and chili sauce, hot bean paste, or red pepper. Cook and stir about 1 minute or till onion is tender but not brown. Add beef broth; bring mixture to boiling. Stir in beef shreds, bean sprouts, and carrot strips; return to boiling. Reduce heat; cover and simmer for 10 minutes (see photo 2, page 19). Ladle into soup bowls (see photo 3, page 19). Top with green onion. Makes 4 servings.

Dashi

When you're in a hurry, substitute dashi-no-moto prepared according to package directions for dashi.

4¼ cups water
1 3½-inch square dried kelp (konbu)
½ cup dried bonito flakes (katsuo-bushi)

In a medium saucepan bring water and kelp to boiling; immediately remove kelp. Stir in bonito. Remove from heat; let stand for 2 minutes. Strain through a sieve lined with cheesecloth (see photo 3, page 15). Store in the refrigerator for up to 3 days. (Do not freeze.) Use Dashi as directed in recipe. Makes about 4 cups.

Chicken and Vegetable Soup

Check the Special Helps section for more information on miso and other ingredients that may be new to you.

4 **cups Dashi (see recipe, opposite)**
1 **whole small chicken breast (about 8 ounces), skinned and boned (see tip, page 34)**
¼ **cup white miso**
4 **ounces taro root, peeled and thinly sliced (about ⅔ cup)**
4 **ounces daikon, peeled and cut into julienne strips***
1 **carrot, thinly sliced**
1 **teaspoon grated gingerroot***
¼ **teaspoon salt**
4 **ounces tofu (fresh bean curd), cut into ½-inch cubes**
1 **cup torn fresh spinach**

Prepare Dashi; set aside. Cut chicken breast into bite-size pieces.

In a large saucepan combine Dashi and miso. Stir in chicken pieces, taro root, daikon, carrot, gingerroot, and salt. Bring mixture to boiling. Reduce heat; cover and simmer for 12 minutes (see photo 2, page 19).

Add tofu and spinach. Cook, uncovered, for 2 minutes, stirring occasionally. Ladle into soup bowls (see photo 3, page 19). Makes 4 servings.

Cleaning Shrimp

Peeling
Starting near the head end, use your fingers to open and peel back the shell on the underside of the shrimp. Then, pull on the tail portion of the shell and remove it.

Deveining
Make a shallow slit along the back of the shrimp. If the black sand vein is visible, use the tip of the knife to remove it. Then, rinse the shrimp under cold running water.

Stir-Fry Cooking

Stir-frying—quick, simple, and exciting. This age-old Oriental cooking method is a snap. Simply follow our step-by-step photos and you'll soon be able to cook like a pro.

Start with a wok or a large skillet. Assemble all the ingredients, then cut, slice, dice, or mince them. Toss everything in the pan, stir a bit, and in a flash you've created a sizzling, crisp-tender stir-fry.

Broccoli in Oyster Sauce

Broccoli in Oyster Sauce

A favorite seasoning in Cantonese seafood dishes, oyster sauce adds a sweet and "meaty" flavor to vegetables.

8	**dried mushrooms**
¾	**pound fresh broccoli**
4	**green onions**
1	**clove garlic**
	Gingerroot
⅓	**cup chicken broth**
1	**to 2 tablespoons oyster sauce**
1	**teaspoon cornstarch**
1	**teaspoon sugar**
1	**tablespoon cooking oil**

In a small mixing bowl soak mushrooms in enough hot water to cover for 30 minutes. Rinse well and squeeze to drain thoroughly. Slice thinly, discarding stems; set aside.

Cut broccoli flowerets into bite-size pieces. Halve any large broccoli stems lengthwise; roll-cut stems into ¾-inch pieces.* (You should have about 3½ cups broccoli total.) In a 1½-quart saucepan cook stems, covered, in a small amount of boiling water for 2 minutes. Add flowerets; cook for 1 minute more. Drain.

Bias-slice green onions into 1-inch pieces.* Mince garlic.* Grate 1 teaspoon gingerroot.* For sauce, in a small mixing bowl combine chicken broth, oyster sauce, cornstarch, and sugar; set aside.

Preheat a wok or large skillet over high heat; add oil (see photo 1). Stir-fry garlic and gingerroot in hot oil for 15 seconds (see photo 2). Add broccoli and mushrooms; stir-fry for 3 minutes (see photo 3). Add green onions; stir-fry for 1½ to 2 minutes or till all vegetables are crisp-tender. Push from the center of the wok.

Stir sauce; add to the center of the wok or skillet (see photo 4). Cook and stir till thickened and bubbly. Cook and stir for 1 minute more. Stir in vegetables to coat with sauce. Makes 4 servings.

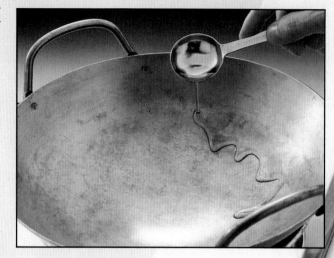

1 Add the oil in a ring around the upper part of the wok so that it coats the sides as it runs down. Or, add the oil to a skillet; tilt it to coat the bottom.

2 Stir-fry the seasonings in the hot oil so that the oil is flavored before the vegetables are added. Stir constantly to prevent the seasonings from burning.

*
See cutting technique, page 27.

3 Using a wok spatula or a long-handled spoon in each hand, lift and turn the vegetables constantly. Stir-frying cooks the food quickly and evenly.

4 With the vegetables pushed up the side of the wok, add the sauce mixture to the center of the hot wok. Immediately stir the sauce to keep lumps from forming.

Szechwan Stir-Fried Cabbage

Whole chili peppers add fire to the cabbage as it cooks, but remember to remove them before serving.

1 **medium head Chinese cabbage**
1 **teaspoon whole Szechwan peppers *or* whole black peppers**
  Gingerroot
2 **tablespoons soy sauce**
1 **tablespoon dry sherry**
2 **teaspoons rice vinegar *or* vinegar**
1 **teaspoon cornstarch**
1 **teaspoon sugar**
1 **tablespoon sesame oil *or* cooking oil**
4 **dried red chili peppers**

Chop cabbage into 2-inch pieces. (You should have about 8 cups cabbage.) Crush Szechwan or black peppers. Grate 1 teaspoon gingerroot.* For sauce, in a small mixing bowl combine soy sauce, dry sherry, rice vinegar or vinegar, cornstarch, and sugar; set aside.

Preheat a wok or large skillet over high heat; add sesame oil or cooking oil (see photo 1, page 24). Stir-fry whole chili peppers and crushed pepper in hot oil about 1 minute or till chili peppers turn dark (see photo 2, page 24). Push peppers from the center of the wok. Add gingerroot; stir-fry for 15 seconds. Add cabbage; stir-fry for 3 minutes (see photo 3, page 25). Push cabbage mixture from center of the wok.

Stir sauce; add to the center of the wok or skillet (see photo 4, page 25). Cook and stir till thickened and bubbly. Cook and stir for 1 minute more. Stir in cabbage mixture to coat with sauce. Remove chili peppers. Makes 4 servings.

Bean Sprouts With Carrots

4 **small carrots**
4 **small green onions**
2 **cloves garlic**
  Gingerroot
3 **tablespoons chicken broth *or* water**
2 **tablespoons rice wine *or* dry sherry**
½ **teaspoon cornstarch**
½ **teaspoon sugar**
¼ **teaspoon salt**
1 **tablespoon cooking oil**
2 **cups fresh bean sprouts**

Bias-slice carrots into ¼-inch pieces.* Roll-cut green onions into 1-inch pieces.* Mince garlic.* Grate 1 teaspoon gingerroot.* For sauce, in a small mixing bowl combine chicken broth or water, rice wine or dry sherry, cornstarch, sugar, and salt; set aside.

Preheat a wok or large skillet over high heat; add oil (see photo 1, page 24). Stir-fry garlic and gingerroot in hot oil for 15 seconds (see photo 2, page 24). Add carrots; stir-fry for 3 to 4 minutes or till almost crisp-tender (see photo 3, page 25). Add green onions; stir-fry for 1 minute. Add bean sprouts. Push vegetables from the center of the wok.

Stir sauce; add to the center of the wok or skillet (see photo 4, page 25). Cook and stir till thickened and bubbly. Cook and stir for 1 minute more. Stir in vegetables to coat with sauce. Makes 4 servings.

*See cutting technique, page 27.

Cutting Vegetables

Roll Cutting
Hold broccoli stem or other vegetable at a 45-degree angle to a cleaver or a sharp knife for the first cut. Give the stem a half-turn, then cut again at the same angle as the first cut, as shown.

Bias Slicing
Hold leek or other vegetable at a 45-degree angle to a cleaver or a sharp knife for the first cut. Make each succeeding cut at the same angle as the first cut, spacing the cuts evenly, as shown.

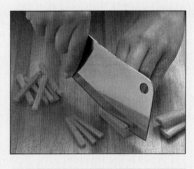

Julienne Cutting
Cut carrot or other vegetable into 2-inch lengths, using a cleaver or a sharp knife. Cut each section lengthwise into ¼-inch-thick slices. Stack a few of the slices together, then cut lengthwise again to make thin strips, as shown.

Slivering
Cut green onion into 2-inch lengths, using a cleaver or a sharp knife. Halve each section lengthwise. (Quarter larger onions lengthwise.) Then, cut each section lengthwise into thin slivers or strips, as shown.

Mincing
Place unpeeled garlic cloves on a cutting board. Using the side of your fist, pound the flat side of a cleaver or a wide-blade knife against the garlic. Remove the peel, then very finely chop the garlic with an up-and-down chopping motion, as shown.

Grating
Hold unpeeled gingerroot or other food at a 45-degree angle to a fine grater. Move the gingerroot back and forth across the grating surface, as shown. Wrap the unused gingerroot in a paper towel. Store in the refrigerator.

28

House Specialties From the Wok

Palate pleasing, colorful, and diverse, stir-frys are the most popular entrées on a Chinese restaurant menu.

In this section we've selected our favorite Cantonese, Peking, and Szechwan stir-frys. Each recipe gives you a just-right balance of flavors.

These dishes are sure to become specialties at your house, too.

Beef and Peppers in Black Bean Sauce

Beef and Peppers In Black Bean Sauce

A Cantonese favorite you'll enjoy at home.

1 **pound beef top round steak**
1 **slightly beaten egg white**
1 **tablespoon water**
2 **teaspoons cornstarch**
2 **teaspoons soy sauce**
5 **green onions**
1 **large green pepper**
2 **tablespoons fermented black beans**
2 **cloves garlic**
½ **cup water**
2 **tablespoons soy sauce**
1 **tablespoon dry sherry**
2 **teapoons cornstarch**
1 **tablespoon cooking oil**
   Red chili pepper, seeded and thinly
      sliced (optional)
   Chili Pepper Flower (optional)
      (see tip, right)

Partially freeze beef; bias-slice across the grain into bite-size strips (see tip, page 35). For marinade, in a medium mixing bowl combine egg white, 1 tablespoon water, 2 teaspoons cornstarch, and 2 teaspoons soy sauce; stir in beef. Cover and let stand at room temperature for 30 minutes, stirring occasionally. (*Or,* marinate in the refrigerator for 2 hours.)

Bias-slice green onions into 1-inch pieces.* Seed and cut green pepper into 1-inch squares. Rinse beans; chop finely. Mince garlic.* For sauce, in a small mixing bowl combine ½ cup water, 2 tablespoons soy sauce, dry sherry, and 2 teaspoons cornstarch; set aside.

(See stir-frying photos, pages 24–25.) Preheat a wok or large skillet over high heat; add oil. (Add more oil as necessary during cooking.) Stir-fry beans and garlic in hot oil for 15 seconds or till fragrant. Add green onions and green pepper; stir-fry about 1½ minutes or till crisp-tender. Remove vegetables (see photo 1).

* *See cutting technique, page 27.*

Add *half* of the beef to the hot wok or skillet (see photo 2). Stir-fry for 2 to 3 minutes or till done. Remove beef. Stir-fry remaining beef for 2 to 3 minutes or till done. Return all beef to the wok. Push from the center of the wok.

Stir sauce; add to the center of the wok or skillet. Cook and stir till thickened and bubbly. Return vegetables to the wok; stir ingredients together to coat with sauce (see photo 3). Cook and stir for 1 minute more. If desired, garnish with sliced chili pepper and Chili Pepper Flower. Makes 4 servings.

Chili Pepper Flower: Cut a red chili pepper** in half, cutting to, but not through, the stem end; discard seeds. Cut each half into strips, leaving stem end whole. Place pepper in ice water about 30 minutes or till the ends curl; drain.
Note: Always wear plastic or rubber gloves to protect your skin from the oils in the pepper. Avoid direct contact with your eyes. When finished, wash your hands thoroughly.

1 Using wok spatulas, transfer the stir-fried vegetables from the wok to a mixing bowl. Set the vegetables aside while you stir-fry the meat.

2 Add the meat to the wok *half* at a time unless the recipe directs otherwise. This prevents overloading the wok and slowing the cooking when you are stir-frying.

3 After cooking the sauce, return the vegetables to the wok. Then, stir all of the ingredients together, as shown. This final stirring evenly distributes the sauce and makes certain everything is hot.

Kung Pao Chicken

To prevent sticking, use a vigorous stir-frying action whenever egg white is used in the marinade, as in this spicy Szechwan dish.

2 **whole medium chicken breasts (about 1½ pounds total), skinned and boned**
1 **slightly beaten egg white**
2 **tablespoons cornstarch**
1 **teaspoon dry sherry**
1 **teaspoon soy sauce**
4 **green onions**
1 **8-ounce can water chestnuts, drained**
1 **clove garlic**
2 **tablespoons dry sherry**
2 **tablespoons rice vinegar *or* vinegar**
2 **tablespoons soy sauce**
1 **tablespoon sugar**
2 **teaspoons cornstarch**
1 **to 2 teaspoons Oriental chili paste**
2 **tablespoons cooking oil**
½ **of an 8-ounce can bamboo shoots, drained**
¼ **cup unsalted dry roasted peanuts**
1 **teaspoon sesame oil (optional)**

Cut chicken breasts into ½-inch cubes (see tip, page 35). For marinade, in a medium mixing bowl combine beaten egg white, 2 tablespoons cornstarch, 1 teaspoon dry sherry, and 1 teaspoon soy sauce; stir in cubed chicken. Cover and let stand at room temperature for 30 minutes, stirring occasionally. (*Or,* marinate in the refrigerator for 2 hours.

Meanwhile, bias-slice green onions into ½-inch pieces.* Coarsely chop drained water chestnuts. Mince garlic.* Set all aside.

For sauce, in a small mixing bowl combine 2 tablespoons dry sherry, rice vinegar or vinegar, 2 tablespoons soy sauce, sugar, 2 teaspoons cornstarch, and chili paste; set aside.

(See stir-frying photos, pages 24–25.) Preheat a wok or large skillet over high heat; add *1 tablespoon* of the cooking oil. Stir-fry garlic in hot oil for 15 seconds. Add green onions; stir-fry about 1½ minutes or till crisp-tender. Remove onions (see photo 1, page 31).

Add remaining cooking oil to the hot wok or skillet. (Add more cooking oil as necessary during cooking.) Add chicken (see photo 2, page 31). Stir-fry about 3 minutes or till done. Push from the center of the wok.

Stir sauce; add to the center of the wok or skillet. Cook and stir till thickened and bubbly. Return onions to the wok; add water chestnuts and bamboo shoots. Stir ingredients together to coat with sauce (see photo 3, page 31). Cook and stir for 1 minute more. Stir in peanuts and sesame oil, if desired. Makes 4 servings.

---

* See cutting technique, page 27.

Pork with Fish Flavor

The sweet and spicy sauce in this dish does not contain fish. Rather, it is made with the same ingredients often used by Szechwan cooks to cook fish—hence the name.

1   pound boneless pork
2   tablespoons rice wine *or* dry sherry
1   tablespoon soy sauce
6   dried wood ears
5   green onions
2   cloves garlic
**   Gingerroot**
¼   cup water
3   tablespoons soy sauce
2   teaspoons sugar
2   teaspoons cornstarch
1   teaspoon rice vinegar *or* vinegar
¼   teaspoon whole Szechwan peppers *or* whole black peppers, crushed
1   tablespoon cooking oil
1   teaspoon Oriental chili paste
1   8-ounce can sliced water chestnuts, drained

Partially freeze pork; bias-slice across the grain into strips. Cut strips into matchstick-size shreds (see tip, page 35). For marinade, in a medium mixing bowl combine *1 tablespoon* of the rice wine or dry sherry and 1 tablespoon soy sauce; stir in pork. Cover and let stand at room temperature for 30 minutes, stirring occasionally. (*Or,* marinate in the refrigerator for 2 hours.)

Meanwhile, in a small mixing bowl soak wood ears in enough hot water to cover for 30 minutes. Rinse well and squeeze to drain thoroughly. Slice thinly, discarding stems; set aside.

Bias-slice green onions into 1-inch pieces.* Mince garlic.* Grate 2 teaspoons gingerroot.* For sauce, in a small mixing bowl stir together remaining rice wine or dry sherry, water, 3 tablespoons soy sauce, sugar, cornstarch, rice vinegar or vinegar, and crushed Szechwan or black pepper; set aside.

(See stir-frying photos, pages 24–25.) Preheat a wok or large skillet over high heat; add oil. (Add more oil as necessary during cooking.) Stir-fry garlic, gingerroot, and chili paste in hot oil for 15 seconds. Add wood ears and green onions; stir-fry about 1½ minutes or till green onions are crisp-tender. Remove green onion mixture (see photo 1, page 31).

Add *half* of the pork to the hot wok or skillet (see photo 2, page 31). Stir-fry for 2 to 3 minutes or till no pink remains. Remove pork. Stir-fry remaining pork for 2 to 3 minutes or till no pink remains. Return all pork to the wok. Push from the center of the wok.

Stir sauce; add to the center of the wok or skillet. Cook and stir till thickened and bubbly. Return green onion mixture to the wok; add water chestnuts. Stir ingredients together to coat with sauce (see photo 3, page 31). Cook and stir for 1 minute more. Makes 4 servings.

Szechwan-Style Pork and Cabbage

12 ounces boneless pork
½ of a medium head Chinese cabbage
4 green onions
1 medium green pepper
1 clove garlic
   Gingerroot
1 tablespoon soy sauce
2 teaspoons cornstarch
1 to 2 teaspoons Oriental chili sauce *or* ½
   teaspoon ground red pepper
1 tablespoon cooking oil

Partially freeze pork; bias-slice across the grain into bite-size strips (see tip, opposite). Chop cabbage into 1-inch pieces. (You should have about 6 cups.) Bias-slice green onions into 1-inch pieces.* Cut green pepper into strips. Mince garlic.* Grate 1 teaspoon gingerroot.* For sauce, mix soy sauce, cornstarch, chili sauce or red pepper, and ½ cup *water;* set aside.

(See stir-frying photos, pages 24–25.) Preheat a wok or large skillet over high heat; add oil. (Add more oil as necessary during cooking.) Stir-fry garlic and gingerroot in hot oil for 15 seconds. Add green onions and green pepper; stir-fry for 1½ to 2 minutes or till crisp-tender. Remove onion mixture (see photo 1, page 31).

Add pork to the hot wok or skillet (see photo 2, page 31). Stir-fry for 3 to 4 minutes or till no pink remains. Push from the center of the wok.

Stir sauce; add to the center of the wok or skillet. Cook and stir till thickened and bubbly. Return onion mixture to the wok; add cabbage. Stir ingredients together to coat with sauce (see photo 3, page 31). Cook and stir for 1 minute more. Makes 4 servings.

Boning Chicken Breasts

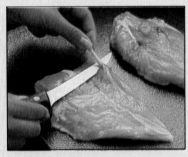

Skinning
Place the whole chicken breast on a cutting board, skin side up. Starting on one side of the breast, pull the skin away from the meat, using your hand, as shown. Discard the skin.

Boning
Cut the meat away from one side of the breastbone, using a thin sharp knife. Then, move the knife over the rib bones, pulling away the meat, as shown. Repeat on the other side.

Removing Tendon
For each breast half, hold one end of the long white tendon with your fingers. Use the tip of the knife to scrape the meat away from the tendon as you pull it out of the breast meat, as shown.

*See cutting technique, page 27.

Peking Lamb
With Green Onions

Create a rich flavor blend with two types of soy sauce.

1	**pound boneless lamb**
1	**tablespoon rice wine *or* dry sherry**
1	**tablespoon light soy sauce**
10	**green onions**
2	**cloves garlic**
1	**tablespoon rice wine *or* dry sherry**
1	**tablespoon dark soy sauce**
½	**teaspoon sugar**
½	**teaspoon sesame oil (optional)**
1	**tablespoon cooking oil**

Partially freeze lamb; bias-slice across the grain into bite-size strips (see tip, below). For marinade, in a medium mixing bowl mix 1 tablespoon rice wine or dry sherry and light soy sauce; stir in lamb. Cover and let stand at room temperature for 30 minutes, stirring occasionally. (*Or,* marinate in the refrigerator for 2 hours.)

Sliver green onions.* Mince garlic.* For sauce, mix 1 tablespoon rice wine or dry sherry, dark soy sauce, sugar, and sesame oil, if desired.

(See stir-frying photos, pages 24–25.) Preheat a wok or large skillet over high heat; add cooking oil. (Add more oil as necessary during cooking.) Stir-fry garlic in hot oil for 15 seconds. Add onions; stir-fry for 1½ minutes or till crisp-tender. Remove onions (see photo 1, page 31). Add *half* of the lamb to the hot wok (see photo 2, page 31). Stir-fry for 2 to 3 minutes or till done. Remove lamb. Stir-fry remaining lamb for 2 to 3 minutes or till done. Return all lamb to the wok. Push from the center of the wok. Stir sauce; add to the center of the wok. Cook and stir about 30 seconds or till heated through. Return onions to the wok; stir together to coat with sauce (see photo 3, page 31). Cook and stir for 1 minute more. Makes 4 servings.

Cutting Meat and Poultry

Bias-Slicing
Partially freeze the meat so it is firm, but not hard. Then, holding a sharp knife or a cleaver at a 45-degree angle to the cutting board, thinly slice the meat. Cut the slices into bite-size pieces.

Shredding
Bias-slice the meat (see photo, left). Then, stack two or three slices of meat together and cut the slices lengthwise into matchstick-size shreds, as shown.

Cubing
Remove skin, bones, and tendon from each chicken breast half (see tip, opposite). Cut breast meat lengthwise into 1-inch-wide strips. Then, cut strips crosswise into cubes, as shown.

Stir-Fried Rice

Thanks to the ingenuity of Oriental cooks, we have fried rice. Though it relies on leftovers, fried rice is one of the tastiest stir-frys ever created.

Bits of meat or seafood and vegetables, seasonings, and cold boiled rice are transformed into beautiful stir-fried masterpieces. Wherever you go in the Orient, you'll find fried rice dishes as varied as the cooks who make it. Here is a sampling of our favorite fried rice recipes.

Yangchow Fried Rice

Yangchow Fried Rice

Fried rice is typically prepared with ham in eastern China; roast pork is used in the southern region.

**3 cups Chinese Boiled Rice
(see recipe, right)**
**4 ounces fresh *or* frozen shelled shrimp
(see tip, page 21)**
**4 ounces fully cooked ham *or* Chinese
Roast Pork (see recipe, page 10)**
½ of a 15-ounce can straw mushrooms
2 medium romaine leaves
1 green onion
2 tablespoons cooking oil
2 beaten eggs
⅓ cup frozen peas, thawed
**2 tablespoons chicken broth *or*
dark soy sauce**

Prepare Chinese Boiled Rice; chill thoroughly. In a 1-quart saucepan bring 2 cups *water* and ¼ teaspoon *salt* to boiling; add shrimp. Return to boiling; reduce heat and simmer, uncovered, for 1 to 3 minutes or till shrimp turn pink, stirring occasionally. Rinse and drain. Chop shrimp.

Finely dice ham or Chinese Roast Pork. Drain mushrooms and chop. Finely shred romaine. Thinly slice green onion.

Preheat a wok or large skillet over medium heat; add *1 tablespoon* of the oil. Add eggs; lift and tilt the wok to form a thin "egg sheet" (see photo 3). Cook, without stirring, about 2 minutes or just till set. Slide egg sheet onto a cutting board. Cut into ¾-inch-wide strips (see photo 4). Cut strips into 2-inch lengths.

(See stir-frying photos, pages 24–25 and 30–31.) Return the wok or skillet to high heat. Add remaining oil to the hot wok. (Add more oil as necessary during cooking.) Stir-fry shrimp, ham or pork, mushrooms, and peas in hot oil for 1 minute. Add rice, green onion, and chicken broth or soy sauce; stir for 1 minute or till heated through. Stir in egg strips. Cover and cook for 1 minute. Add romaine; toss lightly. Makes 6 side-dish servings.

Chinese Boiled Rice

1 cup long grain rice
2 cups cold water
¼ teaspoon salt

If using imported rice, wash uncooked rice under cold running water, rubbing grains together with fingers, till water runs clear (see photo 1). Drain well.

In a medium saucepan combine rice, 2 cups cold water, and salt. Bring to boiling; reduce heat to low and cover with a tight-fitting lid. Simmer for 20 minutes or till small pockets form on the surface of the rice (see photo 2). Remove from heat. Let stand, covered, for 10 minutes. Fluff rice with a fork. Makes 3 cups.

1 If you use imported rice, wash it in a sieve under cold running water till the water runs clear. (American-grown rice should not be washed because nutrients will be lost.)

2 The rice is done when small pockets appear on the surface of the rice. If the pockets contain water, cover the saucepan and continue cooking till the water is absorbed by the rice.

3 Lift and tilt the wok or skillet to form a thin layer of egg, known as an egg sheet. Work quickly because the beaten egg begins to set as soon as it touches the hot wok or skillet.

4 Slide the egg sheet from the wok onto a cutting board. Using a sharp knife, cut the egg into ¾-inch-wide strips, as shown. Then, cut the narrow egg strips into 2-inch lengths.

Nasi Goreng

Garnishes play an important part in Nasi Goreng in Indonesia and Malaysia.

3   **cups Chinese Boiled Rice
       (see recipe, page 38)**
8   **ounces boneless pork *or* beef top
       round steak**
4   **ounces fresh *or* frozen shelled shrimp
       (see tip, page 21)**
6   **green onions**
1   **small cucumber**
1   **medium onion**
2   **cloves garlic**
1   **teaspoon shrimp paste *or* anchovy
       paste**
½   **teaspoon crushed red pepper *or*
       ¼ teaspoon ground red pepper**
2   **tablespoons water**
2   **tablespoons cooking oil**
2   **beaten eggs**
2   **tablespoons soy sauce**

Prepare Chinese Boiled Rice; chill thoroughly. Partially freeze pork or beef; bias-slice across the grain into bite-size strips (see tip, page 35). Thaw shrimp, if frozen; rinse and pat dry. Halve shrimp lengthwise. (If shrimp are large, halve again crosswise.) Set aside.

Bias-slice green onions into 1-inch pieces.* Thinly slice unpeeled cucumber. Thinly slice onion. Mince garlic.* In a small mixing bowl combine garlic, shrimp paste or anchovy paste, and crushed red pepper or ground red pepper; gradually stir in water. Add to pork or beef, tossing to coat; set aside.

Preheat a wok or large skillet over medium heat; add *1 tablespoon* of the oil. Add eggs; lift and tilt the wok or skillet to form a thin "egg sheet" (see photo 3, page 39). Cook, without stirring, about 2 minutes or just till set. Slide egg sheet onto a cutting board. Cut into ¾-inch-wide strips (see photo 4, page 39). Cut strips into 2-inch lengths.

(See stir-frying photos, pages 24–25 and 30–31.) Return the wok or skillet to high heat. Add remaining oil to the hot wok. (Add more oil as necessary during cooking.) Stir-fry thinly sliced onion in hot oil for 1½ to 2 minutes or till golden brown; remove onion. Add pork or beef mixture; stir-fry for 2 minutes. Add shrimp and green onions; stir-fry for 1½ to 2 minutes or till meat and shrimp are done.

Add rice and soy sauce; stir for 1 minute or till heated through. Stir in *half* of the egg strips. Cover and cook for 1 minute. To serve, spoon fried rice onto a serving platter. Garnish with browned onion slices, remaining egg strips, and cucumber. Makes 4 servings.

Nuoc Cham

Vietnamese cooks serve a tangy hot sauce, nuoc cham, as a table or dipping sauce at most meals. Chill any unused sauce.

3   **tablespoons sugar**
2   **red *or* green serrano peppers, seeded
       and finely chopped (see tip Note,
       page 30)**
4   **cloves garlic, minced***
⅓   **cup lime juice**
2   **tablespoons vinegar**
2   **tablespoons fish sauce**
2   **teaspoons water**

In a small mixing bowl combine sugar, serrano peppers, and garlic. Stir in lime juice, vinegar, fish sauce, and water. Makes about ⅔ cup.

*See cutting technique, page 27.

Fried Rice with Sausage and Crab

When you can't buy sweet and pungent flavored Chinese sausage, try using smoked sausage or dried salami.

3 **cups Chinese Boiled Rice (see recipe, page 38)**
4 **dried mushrooms**
 Nuoc Cham (optional) (see recipe, opposite)
2 **Chinese sausage links**
1 **6-ounce can crabmeat**
6 **green onions**
2 **tablespoons cooking oil**
2 **beaten eggs**
1 **tablespoon fish sauce**

Prepare Chinese Boiled Rice; chill thoroughly. In a small mixing bowl soak mushrooms in enough hot water to cover for 30 minutes. Rinse well; squeeze to drain thoroughly. Thinly slice mushrooms, discarding stems; set aside.

Meanwhile, prepare Nuoc Cham, if desired. Thinly slice sausage links. Drain crabmeat and remove cartilage, if present. Flake crabmeat. Thinly slice green onions.

Preheat a wok or large skillet over medium heat; add *1 tablespoon* of the oil. Add eggs; lift and tilt the wok or skillet to form a thin "egg sheet" (see photo 3, page 39). Cook, without stirring, about 2 minutes or just till set. Slide egg sheet onto a cutting board. Cut into ¾-inch-wide strips (see photo 4, page 39). Cut strips into 2-inch lengths.

(See stir-frying photos, pages 24–25 and 30–31.) Return the wok or skillet to high heat. Add remaining oil to the hot wok. (Add more oil as necessary during cooking.) Stir-fry sausages and mushrooms in hot oil about 2 minutes or till sausage is light brown.

Add rice, crabmeat, green onions, and fish sauce; stir for 1 minute or till heated through. Stir in egg strips. Cover and cook for 1 minute. Serve with Nuoc Cham, if desired. Serves 4.

Fried Rice With Chicken

If you don't have shrimp powder for this Thai-flavored rice dish, grind a few dried shrimp in the blender.

3 **cups Chinese Boiled Rice (see recipe, page 38)**
1 **whole medium chicken breast (about 12 ounces), skinned and boned (see tip, page 34)**
8 **ounces tofu (fresh bean curd)**
1 **medium onion**
2 **cloves garlic**
 Fresh cilantro *or* parsley
2 **tablespoons fish sauce**
1 **to 2 teaspoons Oriental chili sauce *or* ½ teaspoon ground red pepper**
½ **teaspoon shrimp powder *or* 1 teaspoon shrimp paste**
2 **tablespoons cooking oil**
2 **beaten eggs**
1 **tablespoon lime juice**

Prepare Chinese Boiled Rice; chill thoroughly. Cut chicken into thin bite-size strips. Drain tofu; cut into ½-inch cubes. Chop onion. Mince garlic.* Snip 2 tablespoons cilantro or parsley. In a mixing bowl mix fish sauce, chili sauce or red pepper, and shrimp powder or shrimp paste.

Preheat a wok or large skillet over medium heat; add *1 tablespoon* of the oil. Add eggs; lift and tilt the wok or skillet to form a thin "egg sheet" (see photo 3, page 39). Cook, without stirring, about 2 minutes or just till set. Slide egg sheet onto a cutting board. Cut into ¾-inch-wide strips (see photo 4, page 39). Cut strips into 2-inch lengths.

(See stir-frying photos, pages 24–25 and 30–31.) Return the wok or skillet to high heat. Add remaining oil to the hot wok. (Add more oil as necessary during cooking.) Stir-fry onion and garlic for 1½ minutes. Add chicken; stir-fry for 2 to 3 minutes or till chicken is done. Add rice and fish sauce mixture; stir for 1 minute or till heated through. Gently stir in tofu and egg strips. Cover and cook for 1 minute. Add cilantro or parsley and lime juice; toss lightly. Makes 4 servings..

Pan-Fried Noodles

Egg noodles—crisp and golden brown on the outside, yet tender and moist on the inside. Sound too good to be true? Pan-fry Chinese egg noodles and taste for yourself.

   Thought to be a forerunner of deep-fried chow-mein noodles, pan-fried noodles are shaped into a noodle cake and browned. Serve the noodle cake topped with any of our delicious stir-fries.

Stir-Fried Chicken with Noodle Cake

Stir-Fried Chicken With Noodle Cake

2 **whole large chicken breasts (about 2 pounds total), skinned and boned (see tip, page 34)**
3 **tablespoons rice wine *or* dry sherry**
3 **tablespoons soy sauce**
1 **teaspoon sesame oil (optional)**
½ **of a medium head bok choy**
2 **medium carrots**
2 **cups fresh pea pods *or* one 6-ounce package frozen pea pods, thawed**
2 **cloves garlic**
  Gingerroot
1¼ **cups chicken broth**
2 **tablespoons cornstarch**
  Pan-Fried Noodle Cake (see recipe, right)
1 **tablespoon cooking oil**

Cut chicken into thin bite-size strips. For marinade, in a medium mixing bowl combine *1 tablespoon* of the rice wine or dry sherry; *1 tablespoon* of the soy sauce; and sesame oil, if desired. Stir in chicken. Cover and let stand at room temperature for 30 minutes, stirring occasionally. (*Or,* marinate chicken in the refrigerator for 2 hours.)

Chop bok choy. (You should have 3 cups.) Cut carrots into julienne strips.* If using fresh pea pods, remove tips and strings. Mince garlic.* Grate 1 tablespoon gingerroot.* For sauce, in a small mixing bowl combine chicken broth, cornstarch, remaining rice wine or dry sherry, and remaining soy sauce; set aside.

Prepare Pan-Fried Noodle Cake; keep warm. Drain chicken, reserving marinade. Add marinade to sauce mixture; set aside.

(*See stir-frying photos, pages 24–25 and 30–31.*) Preheat a wok or large skillet over high heat; add cooking oil. (Add more oil as necessary during cooking.) Stir-fry garlic and gingerroot in hot oil for 15 seconds. Add carrots; stir-fry for 1 minute. Add bok choy; stir-fry for 1 minute. Add pea pods; stir-fry for 2 minutes or till crisp-tender. Remove vegetables.

See cutting technique, page 27.

Add *half* of the chicken to the hot wok or skillet. Stir-fry for 2 to 3 minutes or till done. Remove chicken. Stir-fry remaining chicken for 2 to 3 minutes or till done. Return all chicken to the wok. Push from the center of the wok.

Stir sauce; add to the center of the wok or skillet. Cook and stir till thickened and bubbly. Return vegetables to the wok; stir ingredients together to coat with sauce. Cook and stir for 1 minute more.

To serve, slide noodle cake onto a serving platter. Spoon some chicken stir-fry over noodles (see photo 4). Pass remaining stir-fry. Serves 6.

Pan-Fried Noodle Cake

8 **ounces fresh *or* dried Chinese egg noodles *or* fine egg noodles**
1 **tablespoon cooking oil**

In a 6-quart Dutch oven bring 12 cups *water* and 1 tablespoon *salt* to boiling. Add noodles; cook till tender, stirring occasionally. Allow 4 minutes for fresh Chinese noodles, 6 minutes for dried Chinese noodles, 2 minutes for fresh egg noodles, and 4 minutes for dried egg noodles. Drain and rinse with cold water. Drain well.

In a heavy 10-inch ovenproof skillet with non-stick coating, heat oil over medium heat. Pat noodles in the skillet (see photo 1). Cook, uncovered, for 5 to 6 minutes or till the bottoms of the noodles are light brown. Loosen noodles around the edge, then invert the skillet and noodles onto a large plate (see photo 2).

Slide noodle cake back into the skillet, brown side up (see photo 3). Cook, uncovered, for 5 to 6 minutes more or till the bottom is light brown. Remove from heat; keep warm in a 300° oven while preparing stir-fry. Makes 6 servings.

1 Using the backside of a wooden spoon, gently pat the well-drained noodles in the skillet, making the top of the noodles as smooth as possible.

2 Invert a large plate over the skillet. Holding the plate and skillet together, invert the skillet onto the plate to remove the noodle cake. Then, lift off the skillet, as shown.

3 To brown the other side of the noodle cake, slide the noodles, brown side up, from the plate into the skillet, pushing gently with a wooden spoon.

4 Spoon the stir-fry mixture over the noodle cake. Then, cut the cake into wedges.

Roast Pork with Crispy Noodles

Finely chop the leftover roast pork and sprinkle it over creamy soups or vegetable soups.

1 **pound Chinese Roast Pork (see recipe, page 10)**
2 **small zucchini**
½ **of an 8-ounce can sliced water chestnuts**
   Gingerroot
1½ **cups chicken broth**
3 **tablespoons cornstarch**
2 **to 3 tablespoons oyster sauce**
   Pan-Fried Noodle Cake (see recipe, page 44)
1 **tablespoon cooking oil**

Prepare Chinese Roast Pork, *except* omit serving suggestion. Cut pork into thin bite-size strips. Cut zucchini into julienne strips.* (You should have about 2½ cups.) Drain water chestnuts. Grate 2 teaspoons gingerroot.* For sauce, in a small mixing bowl mix chicken broth, cornstarch, and oyster sauce; set aside. Prepare Pan-Fried Noodle Cake; keep warm.

(See stir-frying photos, pages 24–25 and 30–31.) Preheat a wok or large skillet over high heat; add oil. (Add more oil as necessary during cooking.) Stir-fry gingerroot in hot oil for 15 seconds. Add zucchini; stir-fry for 2 to 3 minutes or till crisp-tender. Remove zucchini.

Add pork to the hot wok or skillet; stir-fry for 2 to 3 minutes or till heated through. Push from the center of the wok.

Stir sauce; add to the center of the wok or skillet. Cook and stir till thickened and bubbly. Return zucchini to the wok; add water chestnuts. Stir ingredients together to coat with sauce. Cook and stir for 1 minute more.

To serve, slide noodle cake onto a serving platter. Spoon pork stir-fry over noodles (see photo 4, page 45). Makes 6 servings.

Beef and Tomatoes With Fried Noodles

1 **pound beef top round steak**
1 **medium green pepper**
4 **green onions**
2 **medium tomatoes**
2 **cloves garlic**
¾ **cup chicken broth**
2 **tablespoons cornstarch**
2 **tablespoons soy sauce**
1 **tablespoon rice vinegar *or* vinegar**
1 **tablespoon dry sherry**
1 **teaspoon sugar**
½ **to 1 teaspoon Oriental chili paste**
   Pan-Fried Noodle Cake (see recipe, page 44)
1 **tablespoon cooking oil**

Partially freeze beef; bias-slice across the grain into bite-size strips (see tip, page 35). Cut green pepper into julienne strips.* Bias-slice green onions into ½-inch pieces.* Cut tomatoes into wedges. Mince garlic.* For sauce, in a small mixing bowl combine chicken broth, cornstarch, soy sauce, rice vinegar or vinegar, dry sherry, sugar, and chili paste; set aside. Prepare Pan-Fried Noodle Cake; keep warm.

(See stir-frying photos, pages 24–25 and 30–31.) Preheat a wok or large skillet over high heat; add oil. (Add more oil as necessary during cooking.) Stir-fry garlic in hot oil for 15 seconds. Add green pepper and green onion; stir-fry about 1½ minutes or till vegetables are crisp-tender. Remove onion mixture.

Add *half* of the beef to the hot wok or skillet. Stir-fry for 2 to 3 minutes or till done. Remove beef. Stir-fry remaining beef for 2 to 3 minutes or till done. Return all beef to the wok. Push from the center of the wok.

Stir sauce; add to the center of the wok or skillet. Cook and stir till thickened and bubbly. Return onion mixture to the wok; add tomatoes. Stir together to coat with sauce. Cover and cook for 1 minute more. To serve, slide noodle cake onto a serving platter. Spoon beef stir-fry over noodles (see photo 4, page 45). Serves 6.

*See cutting technique, page 27.

Cuisines at a Glance

The style and flavor of each Oriental country's cuisine reflects its resources as well as the influences of neighboring lands.

Chinese

Chinese food is commonly divided into regional styles of cooking. Although alike in many respects, each area is unique.

Northern cuisine (Peking or Mandarin) has wheat as its staple grain. It appears in noodles, pancakes, and buns. Other common ingredients in the diet include lamb, tofu, green onions, soy sauce, and garlic.

Eastern cuisine (Shanghai) focuses on the seaport city of Shanghai. Fish and seafood are available, as well as agricultural crops from inland areas. Seasonings are often delicate but slightly sweet. Red-cooking is a specialty.

Southern cuisine (Cantonese) centers on the seaport city of Canton. Known for their stir-fries and dim sum, Cantonese cooks pride themselves on preserving the natural flavor of food, using mildly seasoned sauces.

Western cuisine (Szechwan) is found inland and includes the provinces of Szechwan and Hunan. Highly seasoned and spicy hot, this cuisine makes use of hot chili peppers, green onions, gingerroot, vinegar, Szechwan peppers, garlic, dried mushrooms, and dried tangerine peel.

Japanese

The artistic presentation of food is of great importance in Japan. Japanese cooks insist on freshness in their food and prefer delicate seasonings. They stress seasonal foods prepared in a simple manner. Tofu and shortgrain rice are staples in their diet.

Korean

Korean food has similarities to both Chinese and Japanese cuisines, yet it has a boldness of its own. Beef is popular, as are pork and chicken. Basic seasonings are garlic, green onions, soy sauce, gingerroot, ground pepper, sesame seed, and sesame oil. Rice appears daily, along with pickled vegetables.

Vietnamese

The food of Vietnam reflects the influences of China, India, France, and all of Southeast Asia. Seafood, fresh fruits, and raw vegetables are used extensively. Fish sauce is a universal seasoning both in cooking and at the table. Coconut milk sweetens many dishes.

Thai

Thailand's cooking differs from that of its neighbors in that Thai cooks do not thicken their sauces. Favorite seasonings include chili peppers, fish sauce, shrimp paste, coconut, coriander (cilantro), garlic, and citrus flavorings (lemon- grass and citrus leaves).

Indonesian and Malaysian

Closely related, these cuisines combine spices, chili peppers, shrimp paste, and coconuts to achieve unusual flavor blends. Although not all foods are hot and spicy, their flavor is seldom subtle.

48

Bubbling Hot Pots

Let your guests share in the fun of cooking: Serve an Oriental hot pot. Everyone joins in, selecting and cooking the food in a pot of simmering broth.

Japanese cooks use an earthenware casserole called a *do nabé* (doh NAH bay) and the Chinese cook in a heavy metal Mongolian firepot. An electric wok or an electric skillet makes an ideal substitute.

Chicken and Vegetable One-Pot

Chicken and Vegetable One-Pot

Oriental chrysanthemum leaves add fragrance to Japanese one-pots. Not to be confused with the toxic common flowering plant, shungiku is sold in Oriental markets or can be grown from seed at home.

3 **whole medium chicken breasts (about 2¼ pounds total), skinned and boned (see tip, page 34)**
1 **4-inch piece (1 ounce) fresh burdock root (gobo)**
3 **cups Dashi (see recipe, page 20)**
4 **ounces Oriental chrysanthemum leaves *or* torn fresh spinach**
4 **ounces fresh *or* dried udon (thick white noodles)**
1 **cup enoki mushrooms, root ends removed (about 3 ounces)**
2 **leeks, thinly bias sliced***
8 **ounces tofu (fresh bean curd), cut into ½-inch cubes**
⅓ **cup light soy sauce**
2 **tablespoons mirin**
1 **tablespoon sugar**

Thinly slice chicken into bite-size strips; set aside. Trim burdock; wash and scrub. Cut into thin shavings (see photo 1). Soak in cold water for 10 minutes; drain. Prepare Dashi.

Rinse chrysanthemum leaves or spinach; drain. If using chrysanthemum leaves, discard roots and flowering buds, if present.

In a 4-quart Dutch oven bring 8 cups *water* and 1 teaspoon *salt* to boiling. Snip or break udon into 3- to 4-inch lengths. Add to boiling water; cook about 10 minutes or till nearly tender, stirring occasionally. Drain; rinse with cold water. Drain well. Place in a zaru (Japanese bamboo draining basket) or a serving bowl.

Meanwhile, arrange chicken, burdock, chrysanthemum leaves or spinach, enoki, leeks, and tofu on a serving platter (see photo 2).

See cutting technique, page 27.

About 10 minutes before serving, in a do nabé placed over a tableside heating unit, electric skillet, or electric wok, combine Dashi, soy sauce, mirin, and sugar. Bring to boiling, stirring till sugar dissolves. Reduce heat to simmering. Add *half* of each of the chicken, burdock, enoki, leeks, and tofu; simmer for 4 minutes. Add *half* of the chrysanthemum leaves or spinach; simmer for 1 minute.

Let all use chopsticks to help themselves (see tip, below). Repeat, cooking remaining chicken, vegetables, tofu, and greens.

Add udon to broth. Cook about 1½ minutes or till heated through. Ladle into soup bowls (see photo 3). Serve as soup. Makes 6 servings.

Using Chopsticks: Place one chopstick, about two-thirds of its length from the narrow tip, in the curve at the base of your thumb. Let the stick rest on the end of your ring finger. Close the base of your thumb over the stick to hold it firm. This stick does not move.

Now hold the second chopstick firmly between the tip of your thumb and your index finger, with the middle finger resting on the first stick.

To pick up food, use your index finger to move the top stick up and down, bringing the tip in contact with the tip of the stationary stick.

3 When all of the meat or seafood and vegetables have been eaten, ladle the full-flavored cooking broth mixture into soup bowls, as shown.

1 Using a sharp knife, cut the burdock into thin shavings, as if sharpening a pencil. Immediately soak the shavings in cold water so they won't discolor.

2 Arrange the food on one or more serving platters. To reduce last-minute tasks, clean and cut the food earlier in the day, then cover and chill till serving time.

Mongolian Firepot

1½ **pounds boneless lamb**
½ **of a medium head Chinese cabbage,**
  sliced about ½ inch thick (6 cups)
2 **ounces bean threads**
  Sesame Paste Dip (see recipe, right)
4 **ounces dried buckwheat noodles *or***
  dried fine egg noodles
8 **cups chicken broth *or* water**
4 **green onions, cut into 1½-inch slivers***
2 **tablespoons grated gingerroot***

Partially freeze lamb; bias-slice across the grain into bite-size strips (see tip, page 35). Arrange lamb and cabbage on a serving platter (see photo 2, page 51).

Meanwhile, in a large mixing bowl soak bean threads in enough hot water to cover for 30 minutes. Drain well. Cut into 3- to 4-inch lengths (see photo 1, page 18). Place in a serving bowl. Prepare Sesame Paste Dip; set aside.

In a 4-quart Dutch oven bring 8 cups *water* and 1 teaspoon *salt* to boiling. Break buckwheat or egg noodles into 3- to 4-inch lengths. Add to boiling water; cook till nearly tender, stirring occasionally. Allow about 10 minutes for buckwheat noodles and 4 minutes for egg noodles. Drain; rinse with cold water. Drain well. Place in a serving bowl.

If using a firepot,** about 30 minutes before serving line a heatproof pan with heavy foil. Outdoors, pile briquettes into a pyramid on the foil, then light (see tip, opposite). (The coals are ready to use when they appear ash gray.)

In a large saucepan bring broth or water to boiling; add green onions and gingerroot. Pour into the firepot, electric wok, or electric skillet till *half* full. Keep remaining broth warm; replenish the pot as necessary. If using a firepot, cover the pot. Lower the coals down the firepot chimney, resting them on the grate. Remove the cover.

To serve, give each person a small bowl of dip and a small wire strainer or chopsticks (see tip, page 50). Dip lamb into simmering broth for 30 to 60 seconds or till done. Remove from broth and eat with dip.

After half of the lamb has been cooked, let each person add some of the bean threads, noodles, or cabbage to broth. Cook bean threads and noodles about 1½ minutes or till heated through. Cook cabbage about 2 minutes or till crisp-tender. Remove from broth; eat with dip, if desired. Repeat, cooking remaining food.

Ladle remaining broth into soup bowls (see photo 3, page 51). Let each person season broth with remaining dip, if desired. Serves 6.

**Note: If a firepot is unavailable, use an electric wok or an electric skillet. Omit directions for using briquettes.

Sesame Paste Dip

Freeze leftover dip to use another time.

⅓ **cup sesame paste, Sesame Paste**
  (see tip, page 11), *or* peanut butter
2 **tablespoons fermented bean curd (red),**
  drained; fermented bean curd with
  chili, drained; *or* sweet red bean
  paste
2 **tablespoons soy sauce**
1 **tablespoon sesame oil *or* cooking oil**
1 **tablespoon chili oil *or* Chili Oil**
  (see tip, page 11)
1 **to 2 teaspoons Oriental chili sauce *or***
  ½ teaspoon ground red pepper

In a food processor bowl or a blender container place sesame paste or peanut butter, fermented bean curd or bean paste, soy sauce, sesame oil or cooking oil, chili oil, chili sauce or red pepper, and ¼ cup *water*. Cover; process or blend till smooth. Makes about 1 cup.

*See cutting technique, page 27.

Cantonese Firepot

8 **ounces beef top round steak**
1 **whole medium chicken breast**
 (about 12 ounces), skinned and boned
 (see tip, page 34)
8 **ounces fresh *or* frozen shrimp in shells**
4 **ounces fresh *or* frozen scallops**
 Soy-Vinegar Sauce
 Hot Mustard Sauce (see recipe, page 10)
4 **ounces fresh *or* dried Chinese egg**
 noodles *or* fine egg noodles
4 **ounces tofu (fresh bean curd), cut**
 into ½-inch cubes
3 **cups sliced bok choy**
3 **cups sliced romaine**
3 **cups torn fresh spinach**
1 **cup torn watercress**
8 **cups chicken broth**

Partially freeze beef; bias-slice across the grain into bite-size strips (see tip, page 35). Thinly slice chicken into bite-size strips. Thaw shrimp and scallops, if frozen. Shell and devein shrimp (see tip, page 21). Halve shrimp lengthwise. Halve large scallops. Arrange beef, chicken, shrimp, and scallops on a serving platter (see photo 2, page 51). Prepare sauces; set aside.

Bring 8 cups *water* and 1 teaspoon *salt* to boiling. Snip or break noodles into 3- to 4-inch lengths. Add to boiling water; cook till nearly tender, stirring occasionally. Allow 4 minutes for fresh Chinese noodles, 6 minutes for dried Chinese noodles, 2 minutes for fresh egg noodles, and 4 minutes for dried egg noodles. Drain; rinse with cold water. Drain well. Place in a serving bowl. Arrange tofu and greens on a serving platter.

If using a firepot,** about 30 minutes before serving line a heatproof pan with heavy foil. Outdoors, pile briquettes into a pyramid on the foil, then light (see tip, right). (The coals are ready to use when they appear ash gray.) In a large saucepan bring broth to boiling. Pour into the firepot, electric wok, or electric skillet till *half* full. Keep remaining broth warm; replenish the

pot as necessary. If using a firepot, cover the pot. Lower the coals down the firepot chimney, resting them on the grate. Remove the cover.

To serve, give each person a small bowl of *each* sauce and a small wire strainer or chopsticks (see tip, page 50). Dip meat or seafood into simmering broth till done. Allow 30 to 60 seconds for beef, 1 to 2 minutes for chicken, and 2½ to 3 minutes for seafood. Remove from broth; eat with sauces. After half of the meat and seafood has been cooked, let each person add some of the tofu or greens to broth. Cook tofu, romaine, spinach, and watercress about 1½ minutes or till heated through. Cook bok choy about 3 minutes or till crisp-tender. Remove from broth; eat with sauces. Repeat, cooking remaining meat, seafood, tofu, and greens. Add noodles to broth. Cook for 1½ minutes or till heated through. Ladle into soup bowls (see photo 3, page 51). Makes 6 servings.

Soy-Vinegar Sauce: Mix ⅓ cup *soy sauce,* ⅓ cup *Chinese black vinegar or rice vinegar,* and 1 *green onion,* thinly sliced. Makes ⅔ cup.

**Note: If a firepot is unavailable, use an electric wok or an electric skillet. Omit directions for using briquettes.

Firepot Safety
● **Always use a firepot outdoors because the coals produce toxic gases as they burn.**
● **To prevent damage to the pot, lower the coals down the firepot chimney onto the grate *after* adding the hot broth to the pot.**
● **Add more coals every 20 to 30 minutes, if needed.**

Delectable Egg Dumplings

Petite and omelet-shaped, these egg dumplings burst with a savory filling. In China, the bright yellow color of the dumplings is likened to gold coins. According to Chinese lore, serving these tender morsels conveys a wish for prosperity to all who enjoy them. So, flatter your friends with a platter of good wishes.

Egg Dumplings with Pork

Egg Dumplings With Pork

1 teaspoon dried shrimp
½ cup finely chopped cooked pork
1 green onion, thinly sliced
2 tablespoons soy sauce
1 tablespoon cornstarch
1 tablespoon rice wine *or* dry sherry
1 clove garlic, minced*
¾ cup chicken broth
2 teaspoons cornstarch
½ teaspoon sugar
4 eggs
   Cooking oil
1 teaspoon grated gingerroot*
10 ounces torn fresh spinach
1 teaspoon sesame oil (optional)

In a small mixing bowl soak dried shrimp in enough hot water to cover for 30 minutes. Drain shrimp and chop finely.

For filling, in a small mixing bowl combine shrimp, pork, green onion, *1 tablespoon* of the soy sauce, 1 tablespoon cornstarch, rice wine or dry sherry, and garlic; mix well. Set aside.

For sauce, in a small mixing bowl combine remaining soy sauce, chicken broth, 2 teaspoons cornstarch, and sugar; set aside. In a medium mixing bowl beat eggs.

Preheat a small skillet over medium heat; add *2 teaspoons* cooking oil. For each dumpling, add *1 tablespoon* of the eggs. Using a spatula, shape egg into a 3- to 4-inch circle (see photo 1). When egg is just set, place *1 rounded teaspoon* of the filling on half of the circle (see photo 2). Fold the other half over the filling (see photo 3). Press the edges together to seal. Remove dumpling. Repeat with remaining eggs and filling, making a total of 16 dumplings. (Add more cooking oil as necessary during cooking.)

(See stir-frying photos, pages 24–25.) Heat a large skillet over high heat. Add *1 tablespoon* cooking oil. Stir-fry gingerroot for 15 seconds. Add spinach; stir-fry for 30 seconds. Sprinkle with sesame oil, if desired; stir-fry for 30 seconds to 1 minute more or just till limp (see photo 4). Arrange spinach around the edge of a serving platter; keep warm.

Return the large skillet to high heat. Stir sauce; add to the skillet. Cook and stir till thickened and bubbly; reduce heat to medium. Add dumplings. Stir gently to coat with sauce. Simmer, covered, for 1 to 2 minutes or till heated through. Spoon dumplings onto the center of the serving platter. Makes 4 servings.

1 Using a spatula, shape the beaten egg into a thin circle, keeping the edges smooth and round. Work quickly before the egg sets.

2 When the egg is just set but still wet in appearance, spoon a little of the pork filling on half of the egg-circle in the skillet.

*See cutting technique, page 27.

3 To fold each dumpling, use a spatula to quickly lift the unfilled half of the egg-circle over the filling, forming a half-circle.

4 When the spinach begins to appear limp, immediately remove it from the heat. The leaves should not be completely wilted.

Sensational Sushi

Introduce a popular Japanese tradition in your home—sushi (TSOO shee). A delightful experience not soon forgotten, sushi, or "vinegared rice," is shaped and wrapped with fish or seaweed.

The Japanese use raw, cooked, or smoked fish and seafood to fashion a multitude of satisfying cold snacks. Two favorite versions we've chosen feature cooked shrimp and smoked salmon.

Makizushi

Nigirizushi

Makizushi

Makizushi (MAH kee tsoo shee) means "rolled sushi."

2 **recipes Vinegared Rice**
   Omelet Roll
3 **ounces sliced smoked red salmon**
6 **sheets nori seaweed (each about**
   8 inches square)
1 **small cucumber, seeded and cut into**
   julienne strips* *or* 2 ounces fresh
   whole green beans, cooked (½ cup)
1 **small carrot, cut into julienne strips***
   and cooked

Prepare Vinegared Rice and Omelet Roll. Cut salmon into ¼-inch-thick strips. To toast seaweed, place *each* sheet 5 to 6 inches from the broiler or hold over a gas range burner for 8 to 10 seconds on one side or till color changes to green (see photo 2). Spread *about ½ cup* of the rice over *each* sheet, spreading to within 1 inch of *one* edge and to the other 3 edges.

Center 3 or 4 salmon strips, an Omelet Roll, and/or vegetables on rice atop *each* seaweed sheet. Mix and match fillings, as desired. Starting opposite the side that has rice spread to within 1 inch of the edge, roll up *each* sheet jelly-roll style (see photo 3). Press edges together. Slice *each* roll into 6 pieces. Makes 36.

Vinegared Rice: Wash ½ cup *short grain rice* under cold running water, rubbing grains together with fingers, till water runs clear. Drain. In a medium saucepan combine rice, 1 cup *cold water,* and ¼ teaspoon *salt.* Bring to boiling; reduce heat to low and cover with a tight-fitting lid. Simmer for 15 minutes. Remove from heat; stir in 4 teaspoons *rice vinegar or white vinegar,* 1 tablespoon *sugar,* and 1 tablespoon *mirin or dry sherry.* Cover; cool to room temperature. Use as directed in recipe. Makes 1½ cups.

Omelet Roll: Beat 1 *egg* with 1 tablespoon *water.* Pour into a lightly greased 8-inch skillet; lift and tilt the skillet to spread evenly. Cook over medium heat for 1½ to 2 minutes or till set. Omelet may start to brown. Do not turn. Remove from the pan; cool. Trim omelet (see photo 1). Roll up jelly-roll style. Makes 1.

*See cutting technique, page 27.

1 When the omelet is thoroughly cooled, use a sharp knife or a cleaver to cut away two of its opposite curved edges so it resembles a rectangle.

2 To enhance the seaweed's flavor, lightly toast each sheet on one side only till the color changes to green. Toasting it too long causes the seaweed to lose its flavor and aroma.

3 To make Makizushi, roll the desired combination of fillings, rice, and toasted seaweed together jelly-roll style. The stickiness of the rice mixture holds the roll together.

Nigirizushi

Often made with cooked shrimp called ebi, Nigiri (nee-GEE ree tsoo shee) refers to sushi that is "pressed in the hand."

**1   recipe Vinegared Rice
        (see recipe, opposite)**
**1   pound fresh *or* frozen medium shrimp in
        shells (24 per pound)**
2   tablespoons wasabi powder
1   tablespoon rice vinegar *or* white vinegar

Prepare Vinegared Rice; set aside. Thaw shrimp, if frozen. To prevent shrimp from curling, insert a wooden toothpick between the shell and the flesh on the underside of each shrimp.

Bring 3 cups *water* and 1 teaspoon *salt* to boiling; add shrimp. Return to boiling; reduce heat and simmer, uncovered, for 1 to 3 minutes or till shrimp turn pink, stirring occasionally. Rinse and drain; cool slightly. Remove toothpicks; peel and devein shrimp, leaving tails intact (see tip, page 21). To butterfly shrimp, make a deep slit along the back or the underside of each shrimp; spread sides apart on a flat surface.

In a small mixing bowl stir wasabi powder into 2 tablespoons *water;* set aside. In another small mixing bowl combine ½ cup *water* and rice vinegar or white vinegar.

To shape rice, press a little rice firmly into a 1-tablespoon measure. Invert onto waxed paper. (Moisten fingers with water-vinegar mixture as needed.) Shape rice into a ½-inch-thick oval (see photo 1). Repeat with remaining rice, making a total of 24.

Using index finger, spread a *very thin* streak of wasabi mixture along the split side of *1* of the shrimp (see photo 2). Place shrimp over rice oval, pressing rice and shrimp together. Repeat with remaining shrimp and rice. Serve with *soy sauce* and *pink pickled ginger,* if desired.

To eat, place fingers on shrimp with thumb under rice. Turn upside down; dip only shrimp into soy sauce, if desired (see photo 3). Serve with pickled ginger, if desired. Makes 24.

1 To make Nigirizushi, shape the rice into a thick oval in one hand, using the fingers of your other hand. (For best results, prepare the rice only a few hours before shaping.)

2 Spread a small amount of the wasabi (wah SAH bee) mixture inside the open shrimp. Known as Japanese horseradish, wasabi is appropriately called tears in sushi bars.

3 To enjoy Nigirizushi, dip only the shrimp into the soy sauce. If the rice gets wet, it will crumble. Freshen your palate between bites of sushi with a little pickled ginger, if desired.

Over the Fire

Break out of your backyard grilling routine of burgers, chicken, and steak. Light a fire and add the flavor of the Orient to your outdoor cooking. The grilling know-how is no different than for regular backyard cooking. The difference is in the zesty marinades and spicy basting sauces.

To get you off to a blazing start, we show you how to skewer a saté, baste with sake, and dip into an exotic peanut sauce.

Chicken Saté with Peanut Saté Sauce

Thai Chicken Saté

Spicy satés call for cool, crisp relishes, such as Cucumber Salad (see recipe, page 66). Halve the salad or chill the extra to serve later.

¾	**cup Coconut Milk *or* canned coconut milk (gata)**
2	**cloves garlic, minced***
1	**tablespoon grated gingerroot***
1	**tablespoon fish sauce**
1	**teaspoon finely shredded lemon peel**
½	**teaspoon ground turmeric**
¼	**teaspoon ground coriander**
¼	**teaspoon crushed red pepper**
2	**whole large chicken breasts (about 2 pounds total), skinned and boned (see tip, page 34)**
	Peanut Dipping Sauce (optional) (see recipe, right)

Soak 8 short bamboo skewers in hot water for at least 3 hours. (*Or,* use metal skewers and omit soaking.) Prepare Coconut Milk. For marinade, in a small mixing bowl combine Coconut Milk, garlic, gingerroot, fish sauce, lemon peel, turmeric, coriander, and red pepper.

Cut chicken into 2x½-inch strips. Loosely thread strips accordion-style onto the skewers (see photo 1). Place in a large shallow dish; pour marinade over all. Cover; marinate in the refrigerator for 2 hours, turning often and spooning marinade over chicken.

Pile briquettes into a pyramid in the center of the firebox, then light. After heating, arrange the coals in a single layer (see photo 2). Test the temperature for *medium-hot* coals, using a 3-second count.

Meanwhile, prepare Peanut Dipping Sauce, if desired. Drain chicken, reserving marinade. Grill, uncovered, directly over *medium-hot* coals for 5 to 7 minutes or till chicken is tender, turning and brushing often with reserved marinade (see photo 3). Serve with Peanut Dipping Sauce, if desired. Makes 4 servings.

Coconut Milk: In a medium mixing bowl combine 1 cup *boiling water* and ¾ cup grated *unsweetened coconut;*** let stand for 5 minutes. Place in a blender container or food processor bowl; cover and blend or process for 1 minute. Strain through cheesecloth, pressing mixture to squeeze out as much liquid as possible. Cover and store in the refrigerator for up to 3 days. Makes about ¾ cup.

****Note:** Look for unsweetened coconut in Oriental markets or health food stores.

Peanut Dipping Sauce

Offer warm and pungent peanut dip with any of the satés in this chapter.

⅓	**cup chopped onion**
1	**clove garlic, minced***
2	**to 3 tablespoons cooking oil**
1	**tablespoon sweet soy sauce *or* Sweet Soy Sauce (see tip, page 11)**
1	**teaspoon tamarind paste**
½	**to 1 teaspoon Indonesian chili paste (sambal ulek) *or* Oriental chili paste**
½	**teaspoon shrimp paste *or* anchovy paste**
⅔	**cup creamy peanut butter**
	Chopped peanuts (optional)

In a small saucepan cook onion and garlic in *1 tablespoon* of the hot oil over medium-high heat till tender but not brown, stirring often. In a small mixing bowl combine sweet soy sauce, tamarind paste, chili paste, and shrimp paste or anchovy paste. Stir into onion mixture.

Add peanut butter. Reduce heat to low. Cook and stir till smooth and heated through. Stir in enough of the remaining oil to make of desired consistency. Sprinkle with peanuts, if desired. Serve warm. Makes about 1 cup.

*See cutting technique, page 27.

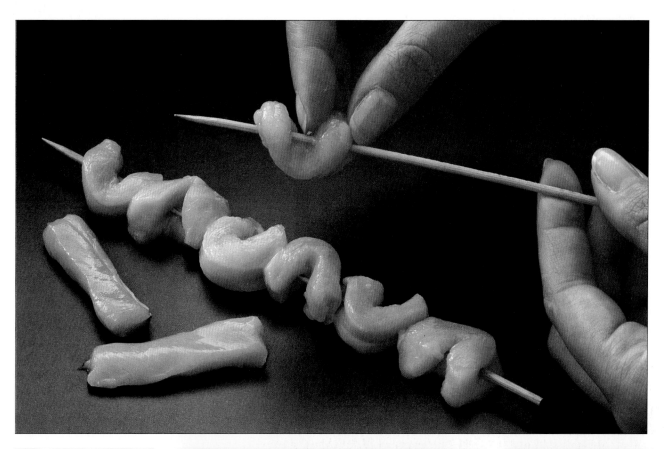

1 For even cooking, loosely thread the meat strips or seafood onto the damp bamboo skewers, as shown. Soaking the wooden skewers in hot water keeps them from burning on the hot grill.

2 When the coals appear ash gray, arrange them in a single layer. Then, test the temperature. Hold your hand, palm down, at the level the food will cook. Start counting "1,001, 1,002," and so forth. If you need to remove your hand after 2 seconds, the coals are *hot;* if you reach 3 seconds, they're *medium-hot.*

3 Brush the meat or seafood with a marinade or basting sauce to add flavor and keep it moist as it cooks. Use a long-handled brush to protect your hands from the heat over the grill.

Indonesian Chicken Saté

Sweet soy, known as ketjap manis, is thicker than the soy sauce you buy at the supermarket, and it has a molasseslike flavor.

**Cucumber Salad (optional)
(see recipe, right)**
½ **cup sweet soy sauce** *or* **Sweet Soy
Sauce (see tip, page 11)**
½ **teaspoon finely shredded lime peel**
¼ **cup lime juice**
2 **cloves garlic, minced***
2 **whole large chicken breasts (about 2
pounds total), skinned and boned
(see tip, page 34)**
4 **chicken thighs, skinned and boned
Peanut Dipping Sauce (optional)
(see recipe, page 64)
Lime** *or* **lemon wedges (optional)
Saté condiments (optional)
Ground black pepper
Chopped green onions
Seeded and chopped red and green
chili peppers (see tip Note, page 30)**

Soak 16 short bamboo skewers in hot water for at least 3 hours. (*Or*, use metal skewers and omit soaking.) Prepare Cucumber Salad, if desired. For marinade, in a small mixing bowl combine sweet soy sauce, lime peel, lime juice, and garlic; set aside.

Cut breasts and thighs into 2x½-inch strips. Loosely thread strips accordion-style onto the skewers (see photo 1, page 65). Place in a large shallow dish; pour marinade over all. Cover; marinate in the refrigerator for 2 hours, turning often and spooning marinade over chicken.

Pile briquettes into a pyramid in the center of the firebox, then light. After heating, arrange the coals in a single layer (see photo 2, page 65). Test the temperature for *medium-hot* coals, using a 3-second count.

Meanwhile, prepare Peanut Dipping Sauce, if desired. Drain chicken, reserving marinade. Grill, uncovered, directly over *medium-hot* coals for 5 to 7 minutes or till chicken is tender, turning and brushing often with reserved marinade (see photo 3, page 65).

To serve, arrange skewers on a serving platter; squeeze lime or lemon wedges over chicken, if desired. Dip into Peanut Dipping Sauce and top with desired condiments. Serve with Cucumber Salad, if desired. Makes 8 servings.

Cucumber Salad

2 **medium cucumbers**
¼ **cup thinly sliced green onion**
1 **red serrano pepper, seeded and
finely chopped (see tip Note, page 30)**
1 **cup rice vinegar** *or* **white vinegar**
⅓ **cup water**
¼ **cup sugar**
1 **clove garlic, minced***
¼ **teaspoon salt**
¼ **teaspoon ground turmeric**

Halve unpeeled cucumbers lengthwise, then thinly slice cucumbers crosswise. In a shallow dish combine cucumbers, green onion, and serrano pepper; set aside.

For marinade, in a small mixing bowl combine rice vinegar or white vinegar, water, sugar, garlic, salt, and turmeric. Stir till sugar dissolves. Pour over cucumber mixture. Cover and marinate in the refrigerator for at least 2 hours, stirring occasionally. Store in the refrigerator for up to 3 days. Drain before serving. Serves 8.

**See cutting technique, page 27.*

Grilled Scallops

A Japanese snack glazed with a sweetened sake sauce.

1 pound fresh *or* frozen scallops
¼ cup sake
¼ cup soy sauce
1 tablespoon sugar
Lemon wedges (optional)

Soak 6 short bamboo skewers in hot water for at least 4 hours. (*Or,* use metal skewers and omit soaking.) Thaw scallops, if frozen.

Meanwhile, for basting sauce, in a small saucepan combine sake, soy sauce, and sugar; bring to boiling. Boil for 2 minutes or till sauce measures ⅓ cup, stirring occasionally; set aside.

Pile briquettes into a pyramid in the center of the firebox, then light. After heating, arrange the coals in a single layer (see photo 2, page 65). Test the temperature for *hot* coals, using a 2-second count.

Halve large scallops. Rinse; pat dry with paper towels. Thread scallops onto the skewers, allowing a ¼-inch space between pieces (see photo 1, page 65). Grill, uncovered, directly over *hot* coals about 10 minutes or till scallops are opaque, turning and brushing often with basting sauce (see photo 3, page 65). Serve with lemon wedges and any remaining sauce, if desired. Makes 6 appetizer servings.

Shrimp Saté

Spicy and aromatic, this saté is popular in Malaysia.

1 pound fresh *or* frozen shrimp in shells
2 tablespoons sliced green onion
1 clove garlic, minced*
2 teaspoons cooking oil
¾ cup chicken broth
3 tablespoons peanut butter
1 tablespoon soy sauce
½ teaspoon finely shredded lemon peel
1 tablespoon lemon juice
1 teaspoon chili powder
½ teaspoon brown sugar
¼ teaspoon ground ginger

Soak 8 short bamboo skewers in hot water for at least 3 hours. (*Or,* use metal skewers and omit soaking.) Thaw shrimp, if frozen. For marinade, in a small saucepan cook green onion and garlic in hot oil over medium heat for 1 minute, stirring often. Stir in broth, peanut butter, soy sauce, lemon peel, lemon juice, chili powder, brown sugar, and ginger. Bring to boiling; reduce heat. Simmer, uncovered, for 10 minutes; stir often. Remove from heat; cool.

Peel shrimp, leaving tails attached; devein (see tip, page 21). Rinse; pat dry with paper towels. Place shrimp in a shallow dish; pour marinade over all. Cover and marinate in the refrigerator for 2 hours, stirring shrimp occasionally.

Pile briquettes into a pyramid in the center of the firebox, then light. After heating, arrange the coals in a single layer (see photo 2, page 65). Test the temperature for *medium-hot* coals, using a 3-second count.

Drain shrimp, reserving marinade. Thread shrimp onto the skewers, allowing a ¼-inch space between pieces (see photo 1, page 65). Grill, uncovered, directly over *medium-hot* coals for 10 to 12 minutes or till shrimp turn pink, turning and brushing often with reserved marinade (see photo 3, page 65). Heat remaining marinade and pass with shrimp. Serves 4.

Steam Cooking

Take a cue from Far Eastern cooks and steam fish, poultry, meats, vegetables, breads, even desserts. A Chinese cooking method as old as their civilization, steaming preserves the flavor, color, shape, and nutrients of food without adding extra calories to the menu.

To help broaden your repertoire of steamed foods, check the next few pages for new and delicious steaming ideas.

*Malaysian Fish
with Hot Chili Sauce*

Malaysian Fish with Hot Chili Sauce

1   **1½- to 2-pound fresh *or* frozen dressed whitefish *or* other fish with head and tail**
    Green Onion Brushes (optional) (see tip, opposite)
2   **tablespoons fish sauce**
6   **cups shredded lettuce**
½   **cup chicken broth**
1   **tablespoon sugar**
1   **tablespoon vinegar**
1   **tablespoon rice wine *or* dry sherry**
2   **teaspoons cornstarch**
1   **tablespoon grated gingerroot***
1   **tablespoon cooking oil**
2   **green onions, thinly sliced**
1   **red serrano pepper, seeded and finely chopped (see tip Note, page 30)**
¼   **to ½ teaspoon crushed red pepper *or* ⅛ to ¼ teaspoon ground red pepper**

Thaw fish, if frozen. If desired, remove head and tail. Rinse and pat dry with paper towels; weigh fish. Score fish with 6 diagonal cuts on one side (see photo 1). Brush *half* of the fish sauce on fish and in cuts; set aside. Prepare Green Onion Brushes, if desired.

In a steamer place a greased steamer rack over water (see photo 2). Bring water to boiling over high heat. Place fish on the rack (see photo 3). Cover; steam till fish flakes easily with a fork. Allow 6 to 9 minutes for each ½ pound of fish. Transfer to a serving platter; keep warm. Place lettuce on the rack. Cover; steam for 1 to 2 minutes or just till limp. Spoon around fish.

In a small mixing bowl mix broth, sugar, vinegar, rice wine or dry sherry, cornstarch, and remaining fish sauce. In a medium saucepan cook gingerroot in hot oil for 15 seconds. Add sliced green onions; cook for 1 minute. Stir in serrano and red pepper. Stir broth mixture; add to the saucepan. Cook and stir till thickened and bubbly. Cook and stir for 2 minutes more. Pour some sauce over fish; pass remaining sauce. Garnish with onion brushes, if desired. Serves 3.

*See cutting technique, page 27.

1 Use a sharp knife to make the cuts almost through to the bone. This type of scoring allows the seasonings to seep into the flesh of the fish.

2 Add water to the steamer, then place the rack in the steamer to check the water level. (The water should not touch the steamer rack when it boils.)
  When the rack doesn't have sides, as shown, place it in the steamer before the water begins to boil (see tip, page 74).

3 Place the food on the rack so the steam can circulate freely in the steamer.

Green Onion Brushes: Trim green onions. For *each* brush, insert a sharp knife 2 to 3 inches from one end of the onion. Cut toward the nearest end. Rotate onion; repeat the cut till end is in slivers. If desired, repeat on other end. Chill in ice water about 30 minutes or till curled.

Beef and Cabbage Rolls

Indonesian cooks favor banana leaves to encase a bold-ly seasoned beef mixture, but we've used an edible wrapper—cabbage leaves.

¾ **cup Coconut Milk (see recipe, page 64)**
1 **tablespoon cooking oil**
1 **small onion, finely chopped (¼ cup)**
2 **cloves garlic, minced***
1 **tablespoon grated gingerroot***
1 **stalk fresh lemongrass, chopped
    (1 tablespoon) *or* 1 teaspoon finely
    shredded lemon peel**
4 **macadamia nuts *or* blanched almonds,
    finely chopped**
1 **pound ground beef**
1 **tablespoon tamarind paste**
1 **teaspoon ground coriander**
½ **teaspoon crushed red pepper *or*
    ¼ teaspoon ground red pepper**
¼ **teaspoon salt**
¼ **teaspoon ground cumin**
16 **medium cabbage leaves**
3 **hard-cooked eggs, sliced
    Hot cooked rice (optional)
    Sweet Soy Dipping Sauce (optional)
    (see recipe, right)**

Prepare Coconut Milk. *(See stir-frying photos, pages 24–25 and 30–31.)* Preheat a wok or large skillet over high heat; add oil. Stir-fry on-ion, garlic, gingerroot, lemongrass or lemon peel, and nuts for 1 minute. Remove onion mix-ture from the wok.

Crumble *half* of the ground beef in the hot wok or skillet. Stir-fry for 3 minutes. Remove beef; drain off fat. Stir-fry remaining beef for 3 min-utes. Drain off fat. Return all beef to the wok; stir in onion mixture, Coconut Milk, tamarind paste,

coriander, red pepper, salt, and cumin. Reduce heat; simmer, uncovered, about 5 minutes or till most of the liquid has evaporated, stirring occa-sionally. Remove from heat; cool.

Remove the center veins of cabbage leaves, keeping each leaf in 1 piece. Immerse leaves in boiling water about 3 minutes or till limp; drain.

To make rolls, place 1 or 2 slices hard-cooked egg on 1 cabbage leaf; top with *2 slightly round-ed tablespoons* of the meat mixture. Fold in sides. Starting at one of the unfolded ends, roll up leaf, tucking in folded sides as you roll. Re-peat with remaining egg slices, cabbage leaves, and meat mixture.

In a steamer place a steamer rack over water (see photo 2, page 70). Bring water to boiling over high heat. Place rolls on the rack so the sides do not touch (see photo 3, page 70). (Cov-er and chill rolls that don't fit on the rack.) Cover and steam about 20 minutes or till heated through. Repeat with remaining rolls.

Meanwhile, prepare Sweet Soy Dipping Sauce, if desired. Serve rolls with rice and drizzle with Sweet Soy Dipping Sauce, if desired. Makes 16.

Sweet Soy Dipping Sauce

¼ **cup lime juice**
3 **tablespoons water**
3 **tablespoons sweet soy sauce *or*
    Sweet Soy Sauce (see tip, page 11)**
½ **to 1 teaspoon Indonesian chili paste
    (sambal ulek) *or* Oriental chili paste**

In a small mixing bowl combine lime juice, wa-ter, sweet soy sauce, and chili paste. Makes about ⅔ cup.

*See cutting technique, page 27.

Steamed Chicken And Vegetables

Pass the fish sauce for an extra dash of flavor.

2   **whole medium chicken breasts (about 1½ pounds), skinned and boned (see tip, page 34)**
1   **medium cucumber, peeled, seeded, and cut into 1-inch pieces**
1   **medium zucchini, bias-sliced ¼ inch thick***
4   **green onions, bias-sliced into 1-inch pieces***
2   **tablespoons fish sauce**
1   **teaspoon sugar**
½   **teaspoon ground laos or ¼ teaspoon ground ginger**
⅛   **to ¼ teaspoon pepper**
2   **medium tomatoes, cut into wedges**
1   **tablespoon snipped cilantro or parsley**
    Hot cooked rice (optional)
    Fish sauce (optional)

Cut chicken into 1-inch cubes (see tip, page 35). In an 8x1½-inch round baking dish combine chicken, cucumber, zucchini, and green onions. (Make sure the baking dish is at least 1 inch smaller than the steamer rack.) In a small mixing bowl combine 2 tablespoons fish sauce, sugar, laos or ginger, and pepper; pour over chicken mixture. Cover the dish with foil.

In a steamer place a steamer rack over water (see photo 2, page 70). Bring water to boiling over high heat. Place the baking dish on the steamer rack (see photo 3, page 70). Cover and steam for 20 to 25 minutes or till chicken is done. Uncover; stir chicken and vegetables. Top with tomatoes and cilantro or parsley. Cover and steam for 1 to 2 minutes more or till tomato is heated through. Serve with rice and additional fish sauce, if desired. Makes 4 servings.

Microwave Directions: Cut chicken and vegetables as above. In a 2-quart round microwave-safe casserole combine chicken, cucumber, zucchini, and green onions. In a small mixing bowl combine 2 tablespoons fish sauce, sugar, laos or ginger, and pepper; pour over chicken mixture. Micro-cook, covered, on 100% power (HIGH) for 7 to 9 minutes or till chicken is tender and vegetables are crisp-tender, stirring after every 2 minutes. Top with tomatoes and cilantro or parsley. Cook, covered, on high for 1 to 2 minutes more or till tomatoes are heated through. Serve with rice and additional fish sauce, if desired.

Attention, Microwave Owners!

Recipes with microwave directions were tested in countertop microwave ovens that operate on 600 to 700 watts. Timings are approximate because microwave ovens vary by manufacturer.

Lotus Leaf Buns

1⅓ to 1⅔ cups all-purpose flour
1 package active dry yeast*
½ cup milk
2 tablespoons shortening *or* lard
1 tablespoon sugar
1 teaspoon sesame oil *or* cooking oil

In a small mixer bowl combine ½ *cup* of the flour and yeast. In a small saucepan heat milk, shortening or lard, sugar, and ¼ teaspoon *salt* just till warm (115° to 120°) and shortening or lard is almost melted, stirring constantly. Add to flour mixture. Beat with an electric mixer on low speed for 30 seconds, scraping the bowl constantly. Beat on high speed for 3 minutes. Stir in as much of the remaining flour as you can.

On a lightly floured surface knead in enough of the remaining flour to make a moderately stiff dough that is smooth and elastic (6 to 8 minutes). Shape into a ball. Place in a greased bowl; turn once to grease surface. Cover and let rise in a warm place till double (about 1 hour).

Punch dough down; divide into 10 balls. Cover and let rest for 10 minutes. Flatten *each* ball into a 3-inch circle. For *each* bun, lightly brush *half* of the circle with sesame oil or cooking oil. Fold in half to form a semicircle; press edges together to seal. Using a sharp knife, make 2 evenly spaced cuts, ½ inch deep, on the rounded edge. Make shallow cuts in a crisscross pattern atop bun. Place on a lightly greased baking sheet. Repeat with remaining circles. Cover; let rise in a warm place for 15 minutes.

In a steamer place a greased steamer rack over water (see photo 2, page 70). Bring water to boiling over high heat. Place buns on the rack so the sides do not touch (see photo 3, page 70). (Cover and chill buns that don't fit on the rack.) Cover and steam about 15 minutes or till buns spring back when touched. Repeat with remaining buns. Serve warm. Makes 10.

*****Note:** Quick-rising active dry yeast is not recommended for this recipe.

Successful Steaming

When you don't have a steamer, improvise. Assemble your own using a large wok or a Dutch oven.

Choosing the Rack
For a steamer rack, use a round wire cooling rack, a small metal colander, or a foil pie plate with holes poked in the bottom.

Supporting the Rack
The sloping sides of the wok hold the rack above the water. To support the rack in a Dutch oven, invert 3 or 4 custard cups in the pan. Add about 1 inch of water, then place the rack on top of the inverted cups.

Adding the Rack
A rack with sides that are easy to grasp should be filled with food, then placed in the steamer over boiling water. A rack without sides should be placed in the steamer before the water boils. Then, add the food after the water boils.

Adding Water
Check the water level in the steamer as the food cooks. Add more boiling water, as needed. Do not remove the lid during cooking, unless checking the water level or doneness of the food. When you do need to lift the lid, tilt it away from you to allow the steam to escape without burning you.

Steamed Jelly Roll

A yummy orange filling swirls throughout a light and delicate Cantonese sweet.

>   2 eggs
>   ½ teaspoon grated orange peel
>   ½ teaspoon vanilla
>   ⅓ cup sugar
>   ½ cup all-purpose flour
>   Powdered sugar
>   1 10-ounce jar orange marmalade
>   1 tablespoon lemon juice
>   ¼ cup toasted chopped almonds
>   Toasted sliced almonds

In a steamer place a 12-inch *bamboo* steamer rack over water (see photo 2, page 70). Remove the rack and line with parchment paper, making sure the bottom and sides are covered with a single sheet of paper; trim off *excess* paper.

In a small mixer bowl beat eggs, orange peel, vanilla, and ⅛ teaspoon *salt* with an electric mixer on medium speed for 1 minute. Gradually add sugar, beating on high speed about 5 minutes or till mixture is thick and lemon colored and sugar is dissolved. Fold flour into egg mixture. Spread evenly in prepared rack.

Bring water in the steamer to a full boil over high heat. Place the rack over boiling water. Cover the rack with a clean dish towel, then cover with the steamer lid. Steam about 4 minutes or till cake tests done. Remove the rack. Invert onto another dry towel sprinkled with powdered sugar; do not remove paper. Cool.

For filling, reserve *1 tablespoon* of the marmalade. Mix remaining marmalade, lemon juice, and chopped nuts. Remove paper from cake. Spread filling over cake to within ½ inch of the edge. Roll up jelly-roll style. Wrap in sugar-sprinkled towel. Let stand for 30 minutes. To garnish, place cake seam side down, on a serving platter; sprinkle with powdered sugar. Spread reserved marmalade in 3 evenly spaced 1½-inch circles atop cake. Arrange sliced nuts around circles to resemble flowers. Serves 12.

Steamed Eggs With Mushrooms

Savor the tang of Nuoc Cham (Vietnamese table sauce) with this tasty brunch or supper dish.

>   ½ ounce bean threads
>   Nuoc Cham (see recipe, page 40)
>   1 tablespoon cooking oil
>   2 green onions, thinly sliced
>   4 ounces ground pork
>   ½ of a 15-ounce can straw mushrooms,
>   drained and sliced (⅔ cup)
>   1 tablespoon fish sauce
>   ⅛ teaspoon pepper
>   6 beaten eggs
>   Hot cooked rice (optional)

In a medium mixing bowl soak bean threads in enough hot water to cover for 30 minutes. Drain well; squeeze out excess moisture. Cut into 2-inch lengths (see photo 1, page 18). Meanwhile, prepare Nuoc Cham.

(See stir-frying photos, pages 24–25 and 30–31.) Preheat a wok or medium skillet over high heat; add oil. Stir-fry green onions in hot oil for 1 minute. Crumble ground pork in the hot wok or skillet. Stir-fry about 3 minutes or till pork is no longer pink. Remove from heat; drain off fat. Stir in bean threads, straw mushrooms, fish sauce, and pepper. Cool.

In a steamer place a steamer rack over water (see photo 2, page 70). Bring water to boiling over high heat. In a greased 1½-quart round baking dish combine beaten eggs and cooled pork mixture; cover the dish with foil. (Make sure the baking dish is at least 1 inch smaller than the steamer rack.)

Place the dish on the steamer rack (see photo 3, page 70). Cover and steam about 15 minutes or till the edge is done but the center is not quite set. Immediately remove from the steamer. Let stand for 5 to 10 minutes or till the center is set. Serve with rice, if desired. Pass Nuoc Cham. Makes 4 servings.

Silver-Thread Buns

Fancy steamed buns or breads often replace rice at Chinese holiday meals or banquets. A popular choice for such meals is silver-thread buns.

Also called snail buns, silver-thread buns are ingeniously fashioned from threadlike strands of dough to resemble a snail shell. They delight the palate as well as the eye.

Steamed Silver-Thread Buns

Steamed Silver-Thread Buns

Chinese cooks prefer lard for their dough making; you'll find butter or margarine gives you the same delicious flavor and texture.

2¾ to 3¼ **cups all-purpose flour**
  1 **package active dry yeast***
  1 **cup water**
  2 **tablespoons sugar**
  1 **tablespoon butter, margarine, *or* lard**
  ¼ **teaspoon salt**
  ¼ **cup butter, margarine, *or* lard, softened**
  2 **tablespoons sugar**
    Black sesame seed (optional)

In a small mixer bowl combine *1¼ cups* of the flour and yeast. In a small saucepan heat water; 2 tablespoons sugar; 1 tablespoon butter, margarine, or lard; and salt just till warm (115° to 120°) and butter, margarine, or lard is almost melted, stirring constantly. Add to flour mixture.

Beat with an electric mixer on low speed for 30 seconds, scraping the bowl constantly. Beat on high speed for 3 minutes. Using a spoon, stir in as much of the remaining flour as you can.

On a lightly floured surface knead in enough of the remaining flour to make a moderately stiff dough that is smooth and elastic (6 to 8 minutes). Shape into a ball. Place in a greased bowl; turn once to grease surface. Cover and let rise in a warm place till double (about 1 hour). Meanwhile, combine ¼ cup butter, margarine, or lard and 2 tablespoons sugar; set aside.

Punch dough down; cover and let rest for 10 minutes. On a lightly floured surface roll dough into a 20x9-inch rectangle. Spread sugar mixture over dough. Fold dough in thirds, forming a 20x3-inch rectangle. Slice dough crosswise into very thin threads, *each* ⅛ to ¼ inch wide (see photo 1).

For *each* bun, gently stretch a group of 8 threads from both ends till about 7 inches long (see photo 2). Starting at one end, wrap threads in a spiral around the first 2 fingers, stretching dough slightly (see photo 3). Tuck the other end into the top to seal as you remove bun from fingers and place on a lightly greased baking sheet (see photo 4). Repeat with remaining dough. If desired, sprinkle with black sesame seed. Cover; let rise in a warm place for 20 minutes.

In a steamer place a greased steamer rack over water (see photo 2, page 70). Bring water to boiling over high heat. Place buns on the steamer rack so the sides do not touch (see photo 3, page 70). (Cover and chill buns that don't fit on the rack.) Cover and steam for 10 to 15 minutes or till buns spring back when touched. Repeat steaming with remaining buns. Serve warm. Makes about 12.

***Note:** Quick-rising active dry yeast is not recommended for this recipe.

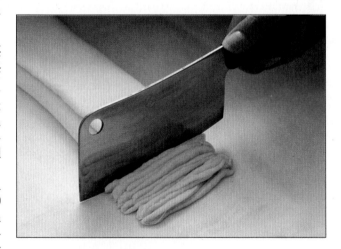

1 On a lightly floured surface, slice the folded dough crosswise into very thin threads or strands, using a sharp cleaver or a large knife.

2 Divide the folded threads or strands into groups of eight. Then, holding the opposite ends of each group of threads together, gently stretch or pull the threads lengthwise till they are about 7 inches long, as shown.

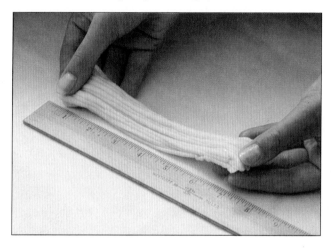

3 Wrap one end of the group of dough threads around the first two fingers of one hand. Continue wrapping the dough around fingers in a spiral, slightly stretching dough as you wrap.

4 When you reach the other end of the threads, use your thumb to tuck the end into the center of the bun. At the same time, slide the bun off your fingers onto a lightly greased baking sheet.

Deep-Fried Favorites

Light and lacy tempura . . . crispy sweet and sour pork . . . luscious lemon chicken. Each of these crisp-fried Oriental delicacies is a well-known classic. The key to their popularity? A special batter that deep-fries to tender perfection without masking the natural flavor of the food.

Tempura

Tempura

Serve this classic as the Japanese do—piping hot.

12 ounces fresh *or* frozen shelled
      medium shrimp (see tip, page 21)
      or scallops
1 small sweet potato, peeled and sliced
      ¼ inch thick
1 cup halved fresh mushrooms *or*
      1-inch cubed eggplant
3 ounces fresh green beans *or* fresh
      asparagus, cut into 2-inch pieces
3 green onions, cut into 2-inch pieces
¾ cup parsley sprigs
   Tempura Dipping Sauce
   Tempura condiments (optional)
      Grated gingerroot*
      Grated daikon*
      Lemon *or* lime wedges
   Cooking oil for deep-fat frying
1 slightly beaten egg yolk
1 cup ice water
1 cup all-purpose flour

Thaw shrimp or scallops, if frozen; rinse. Using paper towels, thoroughly dry seafood, vegetables, and parsley. Prepare Tempura Dipping Sauce and Tempura condiments, if desired. In a wok, deep-fat fryer, or 2-quart saucepan, heat 1½ to 2 inches oil to 365° (see photo 1).

Just before frying, prepare batter. In a medium mixing bowl mix egg yolk and ice water. Add flour; stir just till combined (see photo 2).

To serve, give each person a small bowl of sauce. Pass condiments; add to sauce, as desired. Dip seafood, vegetables, and parsley into batter (see photo 3). Fry, a few pieces at a time, for 2 to 3 minutes or till light golden, turning once. Remove from oil; drain well (see photo 4). Dip into sauce mixture. Makes 6 servings.

Tempura Dipping Sauce: In a saucepan combine 1 cup *Dashi* (see recipe, page 20), ¼ cup *sake or dry sherry*, ¼ cup *soy sauce*, and 1 teaspoon *sugar*. Bring to boiling; stir till sugar dissolves. Serve warm. Makes 1½ cups.

*See cutting technique, page 27.

1 Always check the temperature of the oil, using a deep-fat frying thermometer. Just be sure the bulb doesn't touch the pan.

If the temperature of the oil is too low, the food will become greasy; if it's too high, the food will turn dark before it's done.

2 Use a spoon for mixing the tempura batter. Take care not to overmix or the batter will not puff. (A few lumps may remain.) For other batters, use a rotary beater and beat the mixture till smooth.

3 Dip the food into the batter, then allow the excess to drip back into the bowl, as shown. Fry only a few pieces at a time to keep them from sticking together in the hot oil.

4 Use a wire skimmer or a slotted spoon to remove deep-fried pieces of food from the oil. Drain on a wok rack, as shown, or on paper towels.

Cantonese Lemon Chicken

2 whole large chicken breasts (about
    2 pounds total), skinned and boned
1 cup chicken broth
2 tablespoons sugar
1 tablespoon cornstarch
2 teaspoons finely shredded lemon peel
3 tablespoons lemon juice
    Cooking oil for deep-fat frying
1 beaten egg
¼ cup cornstarch
¼ cup all-purpose flour
¼ cup water
½ teaspoon salt
1 tablespoon cooking oil
3 green onions, bias-sliced into
    1-inch pieces*
1 teaspoon sesame oil (optional)
3 cups shredded lettuce

Cut chicken into 1-inch cubes (see tip, page 35). For sauce, in a small mixing bowl combine chicken broth, sugar, 1 tablespoon cornstarch, lemon peel, and lemon juice; set aside.

In a wok, deep-fat fryer, or 2-quart saucepan, heat 1½ to 2 inches cooking oil to 365° (see photo 1, page 82). Meanwhile, for batter, in a small mixing bowl mix egg, ¼ cup cornstarch, flour, water, and salt; beat till smooth, using a rotary beater (see photo 2, page 82). Dip chicken into batter (see photo 3, page 82). Fry 6 or 7 pieces at a time about 4 minutes or till golden brown, turning once. Remove from oil and drain (see photo 4, page 83). Keep warm in a 300° oven while frying remaining chicken.

(See stir-frying photos, pages 24–25 and 30–31.) Preheat a wok or large skillet over high heat; add 1 tablespoon cooking oil. Stir-fry green onions in hot oil for 1 minute or till crisp-tender. Push from the center of the wok. Stir sauce; add to the center of the wok or skillet. Cook and stir till thickened and bubbly. Cook and stir for 2 minutes more. Add deep-fried chicken and sesame oil, if desired; stir together to coat with sauce. Serve chicken mixture over lettuce. Makes 4 servings.

*
See cutting technique, page 27.

Deep-Fried Phoenix-Tailed Shrimp

A mythical bird, the Phoenix is a symbol of beauty and the inspiration for many Chinese dishes.

1 pound fresh *or* frozen jumbo shrimp
    in shells (about 16)
⅓ cup all-purpose flour
⅓ cup cornstarch
1 teaspoon baking powder
1 teaspoon grated gingerroot*
½ teaspoon salt
    Szechwan Pepper-Salt (optional)
    Cooking oil for deep-fat frying

Thaw shrimp, if frozen. For batter, in a small mixing bowl mix flour, cornstarch, baking powder, gingerroot, salt, and 1 cup *water;* beat till smooth, using a rotary beater (see photo 2, page 82). Cover; let stand for 30 to 45 minutes. If desired, prepare Szechwan Pepper-Salt.

Meanwhile, peel and devein shrimp, leaving tail intact (see tip, page 21). To prevent shrimp from curling, make 5 or 6 cuts crosswise on the underside of shrimp, cutting to, but not through, back of shrimp. Place, cut side down, on paper towels. (Shrimp should lie flat.)

In a wok, deep-fat fryer, or 2-quart saucepan, heat 1½ to 2 inches cooking oil to 365° (see photo 1, page 82). Dip shrimp into batter (see photo 3, page 82). Fry shrimp, a few at a time, for 1½ minutes or till golden brown, turning once. Remove from oil and drain (see photo 4, page 83). Keep warm in a 300° oven while frying remaining shrimp. Serve with Szechwan Pepper-Salt, if desired. Makes 8 appetizer servings or 4 main-dish servings.

Szechwan Pepper-Salt: In a small saucepan mix 3 tablespoons whole *Szechwan peppers or* whole *black peppers* and 1 teaspoon *salt.* Cook over medium heat, stirring constantly, about 3 minutes or till peppers begin to smoke and salt is light brown. Remove from heat; cool. Using a mortar and pestle or a rolling pin, crush mixture. Pass through a sieve. Store in a tightly covered jar. Makes 3 tablespoons.

Sweet and Sour Pork

A yummy Cantonese dish that pairs the sweetness of sugar with the tanginess of vinegar.

1 **pound boneless pork**
3 **tablespoons cornstarch**
1 **tablespoon rice wine *or* dry sherry**
1 **tablespoon soy sauce**
1 **8-ounce can pineapple chunks**
    (juice pack)
3 **tablespoons vinegar**
2 **tablespoons sugar**
2 **tablespoons tomato paste**
1 **tablespoon cornstarch**
2 **teaspoons soy sauce**
½ **teaspoon sesame oil (optional)**
    Cooking oil for deep-fat frying
1 **beaten egg**
½ **cup all-purpose flour**
¼ **cup water**
¼ **teaspoon salt**
1 **tablespoon cooking oil**
1 **clove garlic, minced***
1 **carrot, cut into julienne strips***
1 **large green pepper, cut into**
    1-inch squares

Cut pork into 1-inch cubes. For marinade, in a medium mixing bowl combine 3 tablespoons cornstarch, rice wine or dry sherry, and 1 tablespoon soy sauce; stir in pork. Cover and let stand at room temperature for 30 minutes, stirring occasionally. (*Or,* marinate in the refrigerator for 2 hours.)

Meanwhile, drain pineapple, reserving juice. Add water to reserved juice to make ⅔ cup. For sauce, in a small mixing bowl combine juice mixture, vinegar, sugar, tomato paste, 1 tablespoon cornstarch, 2 teaspoons soy sauce, and sesame oil, if desired. Set aside.

In a wok, deep-fat fryer, or 2-quart saucepan, heat 1½ to 2 inches cooking oil to 365° (see photo 1, page 82).

Meanwhile, for batter, in a small mixing bowl combine egg, flour, ¼ cup water, and salt; beat till smooth, using a rotary beater (see photo 2, page 82).

Dip pork into batter (see photo 3, page 82). Fry pork, 5 or 6 pieces at a time, for 5 to 6 minutes or till golden brown, turning once. Remove from oil and drain (see photo 4, page 83). Keep deep-fried pork warm in a 300° oven while frying remaining pork.

(See stir-frying photos, pages 24–25 and 30–31.) Preheat a wok or large skillet over high heat; add 1 tablespoon cooking oil. Stir-fry garlic in hot oil for 15 seconds. Add carrot; stir-fry for 1½ minutes. Add green pepper; stir-fry about 1 minute or till vegetables are crisp-tender. Push from the center of the wok.

Stir sauce; add to the center of the wok or skillet. Cook and stir till thickened and bubbly. Cook and stir for 2 minutes more. Add pineapple; stir ingredients together to coat with sauce. Stir in deep-fried pork; serve immediately. Makes 4 servings.

Versatile Wontons

Wontons add a lively and versatile note to any Oriental menu. Just vary the filling and cooking method to suit your needs.

When the menu calls for soup, tuck a savory filling inside the wontons and simmer in a flavorful broth.

Need a party snack? Deep-fry sweet or savory filled wontons till they are crisp and crunchy.

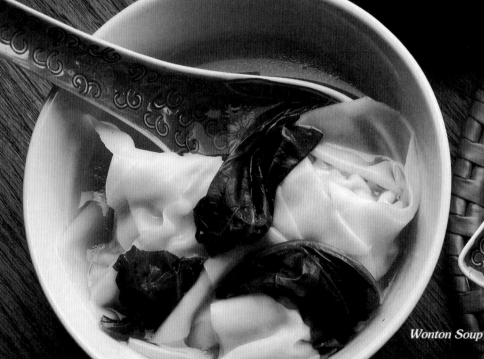

Wonton Soup

Wonton Soup

An excellent make-ahead soup. Fill the wontons and freeze. When you're hungry for soup, add the frozen wontons to the hot broth and cook about 8 minutes.

Pork and Shrimp Filling
36 **wonton wrappers** *or* **9 egg roll wrappers, cut into quarters**
8 **cups chicken broth**
2 **tablespoons rice wine** *or* **dry sherry**
2 **tablespoons soy sauce**
1 **teaspoon sesame oil (optional)**
8 **ounces torn fresh spinach**

Prepare Pork and Shrimp Filling. For wontons, place *1* wonton or egg roll wrapper with 1 point toward you. Top with *1 rounded teaspoon* of the filling just off-center (see photo 1). Fold the nearest point of wrapper over filling, tucking the point under filling (see photo 2). Roll toward the center, leaving about 1 inch unrolled at the top (see photo 3).

Moisten the right-hand corner with water. Lap the right-hand corner over the left-hand corner, pressing together to seal (see photo 4). Repeat with remaining wrappers and filling.

In a large saucepan or Dutch oven bring 8 cups *water* to boiling. Add *half* of the wontons, 1 at a time, to water. Return to boiling; reduce heat. Cover; simmer for 5 to 6 minutes or till pork in filling is no longer pink. Remove wontons and divide among 12 soup bowls. Repeat with remaining wontons. Meanwhile, in another large saucepan or Dutch oven bring broth, rice wine or dry sherry, soy sauce, and sesame oil, if desired, to boiling. Add spinach. Cook for 1 minute or just till spinach is limp. Ladle over wontons. If desired, sprinkle with thinly sliced green onion. Makes 12 appetizer servings.

Pork and Shrimp Filling: Use 4 ounces fresh *or* frozen shelled *shrimp* (see tip, page 21) *or* one 4½-ounce can *shrimp,* drained. Thaw shrimp, if frozen; chop finely. Mix ¼ cup finely chopped *water chestnuts;* 2 tablespoons finely chopped *green onion;* 2 tablespoons *cornstarch;* 1 tablespoon *rice wine or dry sherry;* 1 tablespoon *soy sauce;* 2 teaspoons grated *gingerroot;** 1 teaspoon *sesame oil,* if desired; and ¼ teaspoon *pepper.* Add shrimp and 4 ounces ground *pork;* mix well. Makes 1¼ cups.

1 Spoon the filling just off-center of the wonton or quartered egg roll wrapper. Measure the filling carefully; too much filling will make the wrapper difficult to seal.

2 Use your fingers to lift the point or corner of the wrapper nearest the filling. Fold the point over the filling, gently tucking it under the filling mixture to begin the roll.

*
See cutting technique, page 27.

Deep-Fried Wontons

Pork and Shrimp Filling (see recipe, opposite), Date Filling, *or* **Peanut Butter Filling**
40 wonton wrappers *or* **10 egg roll wrappers, cut into quarters**
Cooking oil for deep-fat frying
Sweet and Sour Sauce (see recipe, page 99) *or* **powdered sugar (optional)**

Prepare desired filling. To make wontons, place *1* wonton or egg roll wrapper with 1 point toward you. Top with *1 rounded teaspoon* of the filling just off-center (see photo 1). Fold the nearest point of wrapper over filling, tucking the point under filling (see photo 2). Roll toward the center, leaving about 1 inch unrolled at the top (see photo 3).

Moisten the right-hand corner with water. Lap the right-hand corner over the left-hand corner, pressing together to seal (see photo 4). Repeat with remaining wrappers and filling.

In a wok, deep-fat fryer, or 2-quart saucepan, heat 1½ to 2 inches cooking oil to 365° (see photo 1, page 82). Fry wontons, a few at a time, for 1½ to 2½ minutes or till golden brown, turning once. Remove wontons from oil and drain (see photo 4, page 83). Keep warm in a 300° oven while frying remaining wontons. If desired, serve pork-and-shrimp-filled wontons with Sweet and Sour Sauce. Or, sprinkle sweet-filled wontons with powdered sugar. Makes 40.

Date Filling: In a small saucepan combine one 8-ounce package pitted whole *dates,* finely snipped; ⅓ cup *sugar;* and ¼ cup *water.* Bring to boiling. Reduce heat to low. Cook, uncovered, about 4 minutes or till thickened, stirring constantly. Remove from heat. Stir in ½ cup finely chopped *walnuts,* ½ teaspoon finely shredded *lemon peel,* 2 tablespoons *lemon juice,* and ½ teaspoon ground *cinnamon.* Cool. Makes 1¼ cups.

Peanut Butter Filling: In a small mixing bowl stir together 1 cup *peanut butter* and ⅓ cup packed *brown sugar.* Stir in ¼ cup *coconut,* 2 tablespoons *Toasted Sesame Seed* (see recipe, page 10), and 2 teaspoons finely shredded *orange peel.* Makes 1¼ cups.

3 Roll the wrapper and filling together toward the center, stopping about 1 inch from the point or corner opposite the roll. Avoid flattening the filling mixture as you roll.

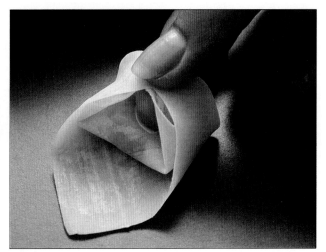

4 Lap the moistened right-hand corner or point over the left-hand corner, pressing the ends together to seal. Moistening the wrapper with water helps seal the overlapped ends.

Crispy Spring Rolls

Deep-fried to a crisp and golden turn, spring rolls resemble egg rolls. The difference is in the wrapper. Our favorite comes from Vietnam. Made with tissue-thin rice papers, these light and crunchy rolls are eaten with fresh herbs, vegetables, and a dipping sauce.

Vietnamese Spring Rolls

Vietnamese Spring Rolls

Carrot Salad (optional)
(see recipe, page 112)
Nuoc Cham (optional)
(see recipe, page 40)
4　dried mushrooms
1　ounce bean threads
1　tablespoon cooking oil
2　cloves garlic, minced*
4　ounces ground pork
6　green onions, thinly sliced
2　teaspoons fish sauce
1　teaspoon sugar
¼　teaspoon pepper
1　6-ounce can crabmeat, drained, flaked,
　　and cartilage removed
1　medium carrot, shredded
10　dried rice papers, *each* about
　　8 inches in diameter
1　beaten egg
　　Cooking oil for deep-fat frying
　　Cucumber, sliced and cut into strips
　　(optional)
　　Fresh mint (optional)
　　Fresh cilantro *or* parsley (optional)
　　Lettuce leaves (Boston, green, *or*
　　red leaf lettuce) (optional)

If desired, prepare Carrot Salad and Nuoc Cham; set aside. In a mixing bowl soak mushrooms in enough hot water to cover for 30 minutes. Rinse and squeeze to drain thoroughly. Chop finely, discarding stems. Meanwhile, in another mixing bowl soak bean threads in enough hot water to cover for 30 minutes. Drain well; squeeze out excess moisture. Cut into 1-inch lengths (see photo 1, page 18).

(See stir-frying photos, pages 24–25.) For filling, preheat a wok or large skillet over high heat; add 1 tablespoon cooking oil. Stir-fry garlic for 15 seconds. Crumble pork into the wok. Stir-fry for 2 to 3 minutes or till no pink remains; drain off fat. Add green onions, fish sauce, sugar, and pepper; stir-fry for 1 minute. Remove from heat. Stir in crabmeat, shredded carrot, mushrooms, and bean threads; cool.

In a shallow dish, dip rice papers, 2 or 3 at a time, into warm water (see photo 1). Remove and place in a single layer on waxed paper; let stand for 2 minutes. Brush any dry edges with a little additional water; cover.

Cut *1* of the rice papers into quarters (see photo 2). On *each* quarter, spoon *1 tablespoon* of the filling along the curved edge (see photo 3). Fold curved edge over filling. Fold side corners toward the center and roll up (see photo 4). Repeat with remaining papers and filling. Combine egg and 1 tablespoon *water*. Brush egg mixture over rolls.

In a wok, deep-fat fryer, or 2-quart saucepan, heat 1½ to 2 inches cooking oil to 365° (see photo 1, page 82). Fry spring rolls, 4 or 5 at a time, about 3 minutes or till light brown, turning once. Keep rolls separated when frying. Remove from oil and drain (see photo 4, page 83). Keep warm in a 300° oven while frying remaining spring rolls.

To serve, let each person place a little Carrot Salad, cucumber, mint, and cilantro or parsley on a lettuce leaf, if desired. Add a spring roll; roll up. If desired, dip into Nuoc Cham before eating. Makes 40.

See cutting technique, page 27.

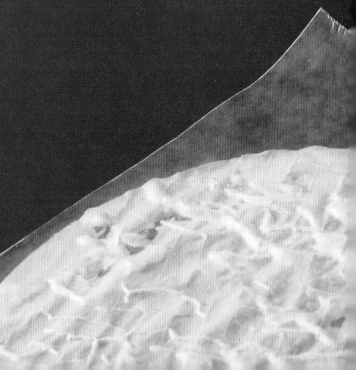

1 To make the rice papers pliable, dip them into warm water in a shallow dish, such as a large pie plate.

2 Use a large sharp knife to cut the softened round rice paper into quarters, making pie-shaped wedges. Keep the remaining papers covered.

3 For accuracy, use a measuring spoon to measure the cooled pork-and-crabmeat filling. Then, spoon the filling in a strip along the curved edge of each of the quartered rice papers, as shown.

4 To seal, fold the side corners of the rice paper toward the center and over the filling. Then, roll the filling and the paper together.

Progressive Dim Sum Party

Dining on dim sum—sweet and savory Chinese snacks, dumplings, breads, even noodles—is a treat usually reserved for restaurants.

The variety of dishes makes a dim sum party at home a bit overwhelming, even for an experienced cook. Yet, we've found an easy way to do it. We've put together a progressive party. That way, your guests share in the cooking as well as the nibbling. And you can have fun, too.

Four-Flavored Dumplings

Four-Flavored Dumplings

Check the timetable on page 98 for our make-ahead suggestions for these eye-catching morsels.

3 dried mushrooms
  Dumpling Dough (see recipe, right)
  **Pork and Shrimp Filling
    (see recipe, page 88)**
  **Chili Oil Dipping Sauce (optional)
    (see recipe, page 100)**
⅓ cup finely chopped fully cooked ham
⅓ cup finely chopped carrot
⅓ cup finely chopped green onion

In a small mixing bowl soak mushrooms in enough hot water to cover for 30 minutes. Rinse; squeeze to drain thoroughly. Chop finely, discarding stems. Prepare Dumpling Dough.

Meanwhile, prepare Pork and Shrimp Filling; set *half* of the filling aside. Wrap, seal, label, and freeze remaining filling for later use. Prepare Chili Oil Dipping Sauce, if desired; set aside.

Divide dough in half. On a lightly floured surface roll *each* half to a ¹⁄₁₆-inch thickness. Using a cookie cutter, cut into 3-inch rounds, making a total of 30. (Reroll dough as needed.) Spoon *1 slightly rounded teaspoon* of the filling in the center of *each* round (see photo 1).

For *each* dumpling, bring 2 opposite sides of round up over filling; pinch together *only* in the center (see photo 2). Pinch together the remaining opposite sides *only* in the center. Repeat with remaining rounds. Enlarge the openings atop dumplings (see photo 3). Place on a floured baking sheet; cover. Chill dumplings in the freezer for 20 minutes.

Remove from the freezer; fill the openings atop dumplings with garnishes, using mushrooms, ham, carrot, and green onion (see photo 4).

In a steamer place a greased steamer rack over water (see photo 2, page 70). Bring water to boiling over high heat. Place *half* of the dumplings on the rack so the sides do not touch (see photo 3, page 70). Cover and steam about 15 minutes or till pork is no longer pink. Remove and keep warm in a 300° oven while steaming remaining dumplings. Serve with Chili Oil Dipping Sauce, if desired. Makes 30.

Dumpling Dough

2 cups all-purpose flour
¼ teaspoon salt
⅔ cup boiling water
¼ cup cold water
2 to 3 tablespoons all-purpose flour

In a medium mixing bowl combine 2 cups flour and salt. Gradually stir in boiling water, stirring constantly. Stir till combined. Stir in cold water. Turn out onto a lightly floured surface; let stand till cool enough to handle.

Knead in enough of the remaining 2 to 3 tablespoons flour to make a moderately stiff dough that is smooth and elastic (6 to 8 minutes). Shape into a ball; cover and let rest for 20 minutes. Use as directed in recipe.

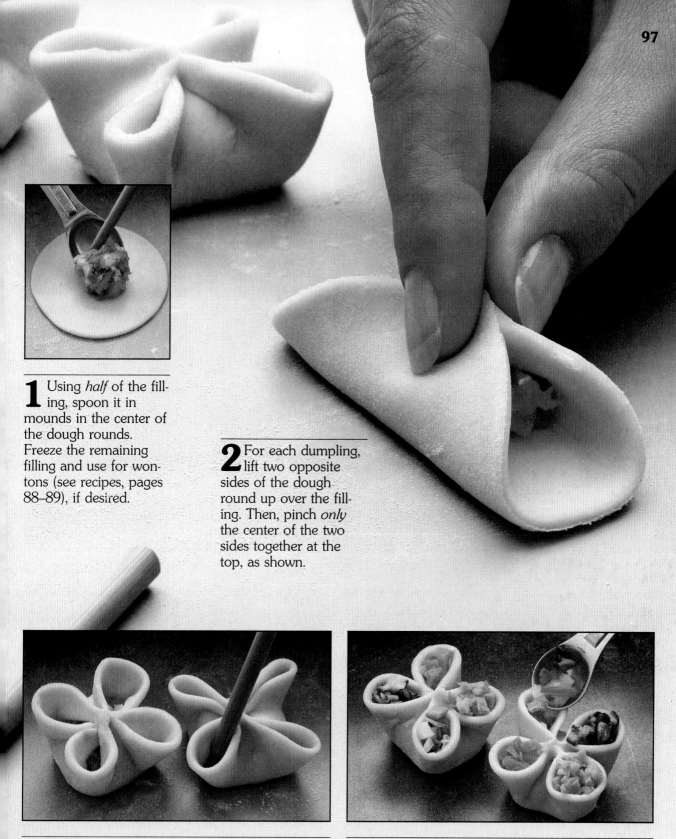

1 Using *half* of the filling, spoon it in mounds in the center of the dough rounds. Freeze the remaining filling and use for wontons (see recipes, pages 88–89), if desired.

2 For each dumpling, lift two opposite sides of the dough round up over the filling. Then, pinch *only* the center of the two sides together at the top, as shown.

3 When sealed, the dumplings should resemble four-leaf clovers. Use a chopstick or a small pointed spoon to enlarge the four openings atop each dumpling, as shown.

4 Before garnishing, chill the dumplings in the freezer, but do not freeze. Then, use a measuring spoon to place the finely chopped garnishes in the openings, as shown.

Timetable

1 st house
- **Four-Flavored Dumplings**.
- A few days before the party, shape and garnish dumplings, as shown. Steam, then cool. Seal, label, and freeze. (*Or,* freeze before steaming.)
- One hour before the party, prepare sauce.
- About 30 minutes before serving, reheat cooked frozen dumplings in a steamer for 10 to 15 minutes or till heated through. (*Or,* steam uncooked frozen dumplings as directed in the recipe.) Serve with a selection of beverages.

2 nd house
- **Chinese Egg Rolls**.
- Three hours before going to the first house, prepare egg rolls, *except do not deep-fry.* Prepare sauces. Cover and chill egg rolls and sauces.
- About 20 minutes before serving, deep-fry egg rolls and reheat Sweet and Sour Sauce. Serve with a selection of beverages.

3 rd house
- **Potstickers**.
- A few days before the party, prepare Potstickers, *except do not cook.* Seal, label, and freeze.
- One hour before going to the first house, prepare dipping sauces.
- About 20 minutes before serving, cook frozen Potstickers in a skillet, as shown. Serve with a selection of beverages.

4 th house
- **Skewered Pork**.
- Three to four hours before going to the first house, marinate pork. Then, thread pork on the skewers. Cover and chill.
- About 10 minutes before serving, broil pork. Arrange on a serving platter. Serve with a selection of beverages.

5 th house
- **Chinese Buns**.
- Three hours before going to the first house, prepare buns, *except do not steam.* Cover buns and chill.
- About 20 minutes before serving, steam buns. Serve with a selection of beverages.

Chinese Egg Rolls

Fill the egg rolls before the party, then chill. Deep-fry just before serving.

8 **dried mushrooms**
1 **whole medium chicken breast (about 12 ounces), skinned and boned (see tip, page 34)**
1 **tablespoon rice wine *or* dry sherry**
1 **tablespoon cooking oil**
2 **teaspoons grated gingerroot***
2 **cups fresh bean sprouts**
2 **medium carrots, shredded**
4 **green onions, thinly sliced**
1 **teaspoon sugar**
1 **teaspoon sesame oil (optional)**
¼ **teaspoon salt**
    Sweet and Sour Sauce (optional) (see recipe, right)
    Hot Mustard Sauce (optional) (see recipe, page 10)
10 **egg roll wrappers**
    Cooking oil for deep-fat frying

In a small mixing bowl soak mushrooms in enough hot water to cover for 30 minutes. Rinse well and squeeze to drain thoroughly. Chop finely, discarding stems.

Cut chicken into thin strips; cut strips into matchstick-size shreds. In a mixing bowl sprinkle rice wine or dry sherry over chicken.

(See stir-frying photos, pages 24–25 and 30–31.) For filling, preheat a wok or large skillet over high heat; add 1 tablespoon cooking oil. (Add more oil as necessary during cooking.) Stir-fry gingerroot in hot oil for 15 seconds. Add chicken; stir-fry for 1½ minutes. Add bean sprouts, carrots, green onions, and mushrooms. Stir-fry for 2 minutes or till chicken is done and vegetables are crisp-tender. Stir in sugar; sesame oil, if desired; and salt. Remove filling mixture from heat; cool.

Meanwhile, if desired, prepare Sweet and Sour Sauce and Hot Mustard Sauce. To make rolls, place *1* egg roll wrapper with 1 point toward

you. Spoon *about ⅓ cup* of the cool filling diagonally just off-center of wrapper (see photo 1, page 88). Fold the nearest point of wrapper over filling, tucking the point under filling (see photo 2, page 88). Fold the side corners toward the center and roll up (see photo 4, page 93). Moisten the top point with water; press on roll to seal. Repeat with remaining egg roll wrappers and filling mixture.

In a wok, deep-fat fryer, or 2-quart saucepan, heat 1½ to 2 inches of cooking oil to 365° (see photo 1, page 82). Fry egg rolls, 2 or 3 at a time, for 2 to 4 minutes or till golden brown, turning once. Remove from oil and drain (see photo 4, page 83). Keep warm in a 300° oven while frying remaining egg rolls. To serve, cut into thirds. Serve with sauces, if desired. Makes 10.

Sweet and Sour Sauce

¾ **cup orange juice**
¼ **cup packed brown sugar**
3 **tablespoons rice vinegar *or* vinegar**
1 **tablespoon cornstarch**
2 **teaspoons soy sauce**

In a small saucepan stir together orange juice, brown sugar, rice vinegar or vinegar, cornstarch, and soy sauce. Cook and stir over medium heat till thickened and bubbly; cook and stir for 2 minutes more. Serve warm or at room temperature. Makes about 1 cup.

Microwave Directions: In a 2-cup glass measure combine orange juice, brown sugar, rice vinegar or vinegar, cornstarch, and soy sauce. Micro-cook mixture, uncovered, on 100% power (HIGH) for 2½ to 3½ minutes or till thickened and bubbly, stirring after every minute till slightly thickened, then after every 30 seconds. Cook, uncovered, on high for 30 seconds more. Serve warm or at room temperature.

*See cutting technique, page 27.

Potstickers

Use ready-made potsticker wrappers as a shortcut.

Dumpling Dough (see recipe, page 96)
1 **tablespoon cornstarch**
1 **tablespoon soy sauce**
1 **teaspoon grated gingerroot***
1 **teaspoon sesame oil (optional)**
½ **teaspoon sugar**
1 **clove garlic, minced***
8 **ounces ground pork**
1 **cup finely chopped Chinese cabbage**
1 **green onion, finely chopped**
  Soy-Vinegar Sauce (see recipe, page 53)
    or Chili Oil Dipping Sauce (optional)
  Cooking oil

Prepare dough. For filling, mix cornstarch; soy sauce; gingerroot; sesame oil, if desired; sugar; and garlic. Add pork, cabbage, and green onion; mix well. Set aside. Prepare sauce, if desired.

Divide dough in half. On a lightly floured surface roll *each* half to slightly less than ⅛-inch thickness. Using a cookie cutter, cut into 3½-inch rounds, making a total of 30. (Reroll dough as needed.) Spoon *about 2 teaspoons* of the filling in the center of *each* round. For *each* dumpling, moisten the edge of the round with water. Fold round in half. Fold small pleats *only* along 1 edge, pressing pleats against the other edge to seal. Place, pleated side up, on a floured baking sheet; cover.

In a 12-inch skillet heat *2 tablespoons* cooking oil over medium-high heat for 1 minute. Arrange *half* of the dumplings in the skillet, pleated side up. Cook, uncovered, for 1 to 2 minutes or till the bottoms are light brown. Reduce heat to low. Remove from heat; add ⅔ cup *water* all at once near the edge of the skillet. Return to heat. Cover; cook for 10 minutes. Increase heat to medium-high. Uncover; cook for 3 to 5 minutes or till all water evaporates. Add *2 teaspoons* cooking oil. Tilt the skillet to coat the bottom. Cook, uncovered, for 1 minute.

Remove dumplings; drain on paper towels. Keep warm in a 300° oven while frying remaining dumplings. If desired, serve dumplings with dipping sauce. Makes 30.

Chili Oil Dipping Sauce: Mix ⅓ cup *white rice vinegar, red rice vinegar, or vinegar;* ¼ cup *soy sauce;* and 1 to 2 teaspoons *chili oil or Chili Oil* (see tip, page 11). Makes about ⅔ cup.

Skewered Pork

12 **ounces pork tenderloin**
¼ **cup hoisin sauce**
¼ **cup rice wine *or* dry sherry**
2 **tablespoons soy sauce**
1 **tablespoon sesame oil *or* cooking oil**
1 **teaspoon sugar**
1 **teaspoon grated gingerroot***
1 **clove garlic, minced***
8 **green onions, bias-sliced**
    into 1½-inch pieces*

Soak ten 9- to 10-inch bamboo skewers in hot water for at least 30 minutes. (*Or,* use metal skewers and omit soaking.) Cut pork diagonally into ¼-inch-thick strips; place in a shallow baking dish. For marinade, mix hoisin sauce, rice wine or dry sherry, soy sauce, sesame oil or cooking oil, sugar, gingerroot, and garlic; pour over pork. Cover; let stand at room temperature for 30 minutes, stirring occasionally.

Drain pork, reserving marinade. Thread pork strips and green onions on the skewers, allowing at least a ¼-inch space between pieces (see photo 1, page 65). Preheat the broiler unit. Place skewers on the unheated rack of a broiler pan. Broil 4 to 5 inches from heat for 7 to 9 minutes or till no pink remains in the pork, turning once and brushing often with reserved marinade (see photo 3, page 65). If desired, garnish with *kiwi fruit, pineapple* wedge, and fresh *cilantro or parsley.* Makes 10 appetizer servings.

---

*See cutting technique, page 27.

Chinese Buns

You'll need a large layered steamer so you can steam all the buns at once. Or, improvise with two or more smaller steamers (see tip, page 74).

3¼ **to 3¾ cups all-purpose flour**
1 **package active dry yeast****
1 **cup milk**
2 **tablespoons sugar**
1 **tablespoon shortening *or* lard**
½ **teaspoon salt**
2 **egg whites**
   Pork Filling *or* Sweet Bean-Date Filling

For dough, in a small mixer bowl combine *1½ cups* of the flour and yeast. In a small saucepan heat milk, sugar, shortening or lard, and salt just till warm (115° to 120°) and shortening or lard is almost melted, stirring constantly. Add to flour mixture; add egg whites. Beat with an electric mixer on low speed for 30 seconds, scraping the bowl constantly. Beat on high speed for 3 minutes. Using a spoon, stir in as much of the remaining flour as you can.

On a lightly floured surface knead in enough of the remaining flour to make a moderately stiff dough that is smooth and elastic (6 to 8 minutes). Shape into a ball. Place in a greased bowl; turn once to grease surface. Cover and let rise in a warm place till double (about 1 hour). Meanwhile, prepare desired filling.

To shape buns, punch dough down; divide into 20 balls. Cover and let rest for 10 minutes. Flatten *each* ball into a 3½-inch circle. For *each* bun, place *2 scant tablespoons* of the pork filling or *1 scant tablespoon* of the sweet filling in the center of the circle. Bring up edges; moisten and press to seal seams. Place, seam side down, on a lightly greased baking sheet. Repeat with remaining circles and filling. If desired, dip a small Oriental rubber stamp or the square end of a chopstick into red food coloring; press atop sweet-filled buns *only*. Cover; let rise in a warm place for 20 minutes. (*Or,* if buns are not steamed immediately after rising, omit rising. After shaping, cover; chill for up to 6 hours.)

In a layered steamer place a greased steamer rack over water (see photo 2, page 70). Bring water to boiling over high heat. Place buns on the racks so the sides do not touch (see photo 3, page 70). Cover; steam about 15 minutes or till buns spring back when touched. Serve buns warm. Makes 20.

Pork Filling: In a small mixing bowl soak 12 dried *mushrooms* in enough hot water to cover for 30 minutes. Rinse and squeeze to drain thoroughly. Chop finely, discarding stems. Meanwhile, in a medium mixing bowl toss together 12 ounces lean boneless *pork,* diced; 2 teaspoons *sugar;* 2 teaspoons *soy sauce;* and ¼ teaspoon *pepper.* For sauce, in another small mixing bowl mix 3 tablespoons *oyster sauce,* 2 tablespoons *water,* and 1½ teaspoons *cornstarch;* set aside.

(See stir-frying photos, pages 24–25 and 30–31.) Preheat a wok or large skillet over high heat; add 1 tablespoon *cooking oil.* (Add more oil as necessary during cooking.) Stir-fry 2 teaspoons grated *gingerroot** in hot oil for 15 seconds. Add 3 thinly sliced *green onions;* stir-fry for 1 minute. Add pork; stir-fry for 2 to 3 minutes or till no pink remains in pork. Push from the center of the wok.

Stir sauce; add to the center of the wok or skillet. Cook and stir till thickened and bubbly; cook and stir for 2 minutes more. Stir in mushrooms and ½ of an 8-ounce can *bamboo shoots,* drained and chopped; remove from heat. Makes 2¼ cups.

Sweet Bean-Date Filling: In a small mixing bowl combine ⅔ cup canned *sweet red bean paste,* ½ cup finely snipped pitted *dates,* ½ cup finely chopped *walnuts,* and ½ teaspoon *vanilla.* Makes about 1 cup.

****Note:** Quick-rising active dry yeast is not recommended in this recipe.

Szechwan Duck

The contrast of crisp and tender is nowhere more delightful than in this Szechwan dish. The secret of this specialty? A pairing of cooking methods.

First the duck is gently steamed. Then it is deep-fried to seal in the juices and to crisp the skin. The result: an extraordinary blend of textures you'll savor with every bite.

Crispy Szechwan Duck

Crispy Szechwan Duck

1 **4- to 5-pound domestic duckling**
2 **tablespoons whole Szechwan peppers *or* whole black peppers**
2 **star anise *or* 2 teaspoons aniseed**
3 **green onions, thinly sliced**
2 **tablespoons rice wine *or* dry sherry**
1 **tablespoon grated gingerroot***
1 **teaspoon salt**
 Lotus Leaf Buns (see recipe, page 74)
2 **tablespoons soy sauce**
2 **teaspoons five-spice powder *or* Five-Spice Powder (see tip, page 11)**
⅓ **cup cornstarch**
 Cooking oil for deep-fat frying
 Hoisin sauce *or* sweet bean sauce
 Green onion slivers*

Rinse duck; pat dry. Place duck, breast side up, on a counter surface. Press down firmly on the breastbone to flatten (see photo 1).

Using a mortar and pestle or a rolling pin, crush Szechwan or black peppers and anise or aniseed; strain, if desired. In a small mixing bowl combine pepper mixture, sliced green onions, rice wine or dry sherry, gingerroot, and salt. Rub mixture over duck and inside cavity. Cover and chill for 6 hours or overnight.

In a steamer place a greased steamer rack over water (see photo 2, page 70). Bring water to boiling over high heat. Place seasoned duck, breast side up, on the rack (see photo 3, page 70). Cover and steam for 2 hours. (Replenish boiling water, as needed.) Meanwhile, prepare Lotus Leaf Buns.

Remove duck from the steamer; discard cooking juices. Using paper towels, wipe duck to remove onion mixture. Let duck stand, uncovered, at room temperature, for 30 minutes.

In a small mixing bowl combine soy sauce and five-spice powder. Brush over duck. Sprinkle cornstarch over duck, pressing lightly with fingers, to coat evenly. Let stand for 15 minutes.

Meanwhile, in a large wok or a 5-quart Dutch oven heat 1½ inches cooking oil to 375° (see photo 1, page 82). Using 2 large long-handled spoons, *carefully* lower duck, breast side up, into hot oil (see photo 2). Fry duck for 8 to 10 minutes or till crisp and golden brown on the bottom, occasionally spooning hot oil over duck. Use spoons to prevent duck from sticking to the sides of the wok.

Carefully turn duck. Fry for 8 to 10 minutes more or till crisp and golden brown, moving duck to prevent sticking. Remove from oil and drain on paper towels.

If desired, carve duck Oriental style (see tip, opposite). Serve with buns, hoisin or sweet bean sauce, and green onion slivers. To eat, open bun; spread with a little sauce. Add a few onion slivers and some duck. Eat as a sandwich. Makes 5 servings.

1 Using both hands, press down firmly on the breast side of the duck to flatten the breastbone. This makes the duck easier to handle when it is deep-fat fried in the wok.

2 Insert a long-handled spoon into the tail end of the duck. Use another spoon under the opposite end to slowly lower the duck into the hot oil, as shown. (Be sure the deep-fat frying thermometer is secure.)

**See cutting technique, page 27.*

Oriental-Style Carving

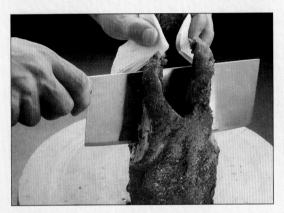

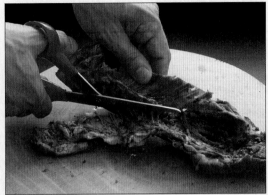

1 Use a cleaver to remove the wings and legs of the duck. Then, with one hand, stand the duck, tail side up. Use paper towels to protect your hand from the heat. Halve the duck lengthwise between the breast and the back, as shown.

2 Use kitchen shears to cut along the backbone. Discard the backbone and the tail. Chop the back sections into 1- to 1½-inch pieces, cutting through the meat and bone. Reassemble the back, skin side down, on a serving platter.

3 Use a boning knife to remove the meat, in one piece, from the breastbone. Discard the collarbone. Halve the breast lengthwise, then crosswise into 1- to 1½-inch pieces. Reassemble the breast meat, skin side up, atop the back.

4 Use a cleaver to separate the legs from the thighs. Then, chop each wing, leg, and thigh into two sections, cutting through the meat and bone, as shown. Arrange the wings, legs, and thighs in their original shape on the platter.

Oriental Dinner Party

You love Oriental food but think it's too much work for entertaining? It doesn't have to be if you follow our lead. We've organized the menu and preplanned the cooking, and we take you step by step through the timetable. After your guests depart, you'll wonder why you waited so long to "go Oriental."

Menu

- Oriental Cold Plate*

- Moo Shu Pork with Mandarin Pancakes*

- Marinated Salmon*

- Pea Pods with Corn*

- Hot cooked rice

- Fruit Platter*

see pages 108-113

*Moo Shu Pork with
Mandarin Pancakes*

Moo Shu Pork with Mandarin Pancakes

Make the pancakes ahead and freeze. Then, thaw at room temperature. To reheat in a steamer, wrap pancakes in a cloth napkin and steam about 5 minutes. Or, layer pancakes with foil on a foil-lined baking sheet. Cover and heat in a 375° oven about 7 minutes.

Mandarin Pancakes
8 ounces boneless pork
2 teaspoons soy sauce
1 teaspoon rice wine *or* dry sherry
4 dried mushrooms
1 dried cloud ear
¼ cup dried lily buds
 Green Onion Brushes (see tip, page 71)
2 tablespoons cooking oil
2 beaten eggs
2 teaspoons grated gingerroot*
1 small carrot, cut into julienne strips*
3 green onions, cut into 1½-inch slivers*
¾ cup shredded Chinese cabbage
1 tablespoon soy sauce
½ teaspoon sesame oil (optional)
¼ teaspoon sugar
 Hoisin sauce

Prepare Mandarin Pancakes. Partially freeze pork; thinly slice across the grain into strips. Cut strips into matchstick-size shreds (see tip, page 35). For marinade, in a medium mixing bowl mix 2 teaspoons soy sauce and rice wine or dry sherry; stir in pork. Cover; let stand at room temperature for 30 minutes. Stir occasionally. (*Or,* marinate in the refrigerator for 2 hours.)

In another mixing bowl soak mushrooms, cloud ear, and lily buds in enough hot water to cover for 30 minutes. Rinse and squeeze to drain thoroughly. Cut mushrooms and cloud ear into julienne strips*, discarding stems. Cut lily buds into 1-inch pieces. Prepare Green Onion Brushes, cutting *only* 1 end of *each* green onion.

Preheat a wok or large skillet over medium heat; add *1 tablespoon* of the cooking oil. Add eggs; lift and tilt the wok or skillet to form a thin

"egg sheet" (see photo 3, page 39). Cook, without stirring, about 2 minutes or just till set. Slide egg sheet onto a cutting board. Thinly slice into bite-size strips; set aside.

(See stir-frying photos, pages 24–25 and 30–31.) Return the wok or skillet to high heat. Add remaining cooking oil to the hot wok. (Add more cooking oil as necessary during cooking.) Stir-fry gingerroot for 15 seconds. Add carrot; stir-fry for 1½ minutes. Add *half* of the green onion slivers and cabbage; stir-fry for 1½ minutes. Remove vegetables.

Add pork mixture to the hot wok or skillet. Stir-fry for 2 to 3 minutes or till no pink remains. Return vegetables to the wok. Add mushrooms; cloud ear; lily buds; 1 tablespoon soy sauce; sesame oil, if desired; and sugar. Stir for 1 minute or till heated through. Stir in egg strips.

To serve, let each person brush a little hoisin sauce on a pancake, using an onion brush (see photo, page 107). Spoon *about* ⅓ *cup* of the pork mixture in the center of pancake; top with a few remaining green onion slivers. Fold filling and pancake envelope-style or jelly-roll style (see photo 4). Eat out of hand. Serves 8.

Mandarin Pancakes: Prepare ½ of the recipe for Dumpling Dough (see recipe, page 96). On a lightly floured surface form dough into an 8-inch-long roll. Cut into 1-inch pieces. Flatten *each* piece into a 3-inch round (see photo 1). To make pancakes, roll *each* round into a 6-inch circle. Lightly brush one side of *each* circle with *cooking oil or sesame oil (*see photo 2). Make stacks of 2 pancakes each, oiled sides together; cover. Heat a heavy ungreased skillet or griddle over medium-high heat. Add 1 pancake stack. Cook for 30 seconds to 1 minute on *each* side or till bubbles appear on the surface and the bottom begins to brown. Remove from the skillet. Separate pancakes (see photo 3). Cover. Repeat, cooking remaining stacks. Makes 8.

*See cutting technique, page 27.

1 Use the tips of your fingers to gently flatten each piece of dumpling dough into a 3-inch round. Work quickly to prevent the dough from drying out.

2 Brush a little cooking oil or sesame oil on one side of *each* circle. This keeps the pancakes from sticking together when they are stacked for cooking.

3 Because the pancakes are fragile, cook them in stacks of two each. Then, gently separate the cooked pancakes, using your fingers, as shown.

4 To fold the filling and pancake envelope-style, bring one edge of the pancake up to overlap the filling. Then, lap the two adjacent edges of the pancake over the filling (as shown, front). Or, roll the filling and pancake together jelly-roll style (as shown, back).

Timetable

3 or 4 days before
- Make Mandarin Pancakes. After cooking, separate pancakes, as shown. Then, cool, seal, label, and freeze pancakes.
- Prepare Kimchi. Cover and let stand in a cool place (60°) for 3 days. Then, store in the refrigerator.

1 day before
- Shred carrot for Carrot Salad, as shown. Marinate in the refrigerator. Prepare Red-Cooked Beef and Asparagus in Miso. Cover and chill.

6 hrs. before
- Remove pancakes from the freezer to thaw.
- Marinate salmon in the refrigerator.
- Prepare fruit and arrange Fruit Platter. Cover and chill till serving time.
- Set the table. Arrange a serving area for guests to help themselves to Oriental Cold Plate and Moo Shu Pork with Mandarin Pancakes.

2 hrs. before
- Prepare ingredients for Moo Shu Pork and Pea Pods with Corn.
- Arrange foods for Oriental Cold Plate on a large serving platter. Cover and chill. Remove from the refrigerator about 30 minutes before guests arrive.
- Measure rice and start cooking it about 30 minutes before serving the main course.

Before Serving
- Reheat pancakes in a steamer or in the oven.
- Stir-fry Moo Shu Pork.
- Offer sake or Chinese beer with appetizers.
- Make tea.
- Place salmon in the oven. Prepare pea pods.
- Arrange food in serving dishes and pour tea.

Oriental Cold Plate

Before dinner, invite guests to sample this spicy assortment, along with Moo Shu Pork (see recipe, page 108).

Kimchi (see recipe, below)
Red-Cooked Beef (see recipe, right)
Asparagus in Miso (see recipe, page 112)
Carrot Salad (see recipe, page 112)
Lettuce leaves (Boston, green, *or* red leaf lettuce)

Prepare Kimchi, Red-Cooked Beef, Asparagus in Miso, and Carrot Salad. To serve, line a large serving platter with lettuce leaves. Arrange desired amount of beef and vegetables over lettuce. Makes 8 appetizer servings.

Kimchi

A Korean mealtime staple: pungent pickled cabbage.

1½ to 2 pounds Chinese cabbage *or* bok choy, cut into 1½-inch pieces (16 cups)
4 cups water
½ cup salt
4 ounces daikon, peeled and cut into julienne strips* (1 cup)
3 green onions, cut into slivers* (½ cup)
2 teaspoons salted shrimp *or* shrimp paste
2 cloves garlic, minced*
2 teaspoons sugar
1 teaspoon ground red pepper
1 teaspoon grated gingerroot*

In a large mixing bowl combine cabbage or bok choy, water, and salt. Let stand for 4 hours. Drain; rinse well with cold water. Drain again.

In the same bowl combine daikon, green onions, salted shrimp or shrimp paste, garlic, sugar, red pepper, and gingerroot. Add cabbage; mix well. Press mixture into a 1-quart jar. Secure lid. Let stand in a cool place (about 60°) for 3 days. Store in the refrigerator, covered, for up to 10 days. Makes 4 cups.

**See cutting technique, page 27.*

Red-Cooked Beef

Savor a sensational blend of spices in this cold meat dish from China.

2 tablespoons dried tangerine peel *or* Dried Tangerine Peel (see tip, page 11)
2 star anise *or* 2 teaspoons aniseed
2 teaspoons whole Szechwan peppers *or* whole black peppers
1 teaspoon cardamom seed
½ teaspoon fennel seed
2 whole cloves
2 cups water
1 cup soy sauce
⅓ cup sugar
1 2-pound beef bottom round roast

For spice bag, wrap tangerine peel, star anise or aniseed, Szechwan or black peppers, cardamom, fennel, and cloves in cheesecloth (see photo 1, page 14). In a 4-quart Dutch oven combine water, soy sauce, sugar, and spice bag. Bring to boiling.

Trim excess fat from meat. Place meat in soy mixture. Return to boiling; reduce heat. Cover and simmer for 45 minutes.

Turn meat. Simmer, covered, for 45 to 55 minutes more or till meat is tender, basting often with cooking liquid during the last 10 minutes (see photo 2, page 14).

Remove meat from pan, reserving cooking liquid. When cool enough to handle, cover meat and chill. Strain reserved liquid and discard spice bag (see photo 3, page 14). Skim fat from liquid. Store liquid in the refrigerator for up to 3 days or in the freezer for up to 6 months. Reuse for other red-cooked dishes or pass with cold meat, if desired.

To serve, cut meat across the grain into ⅛-inch-thick slices. Serve as part of a cold plate or use in sandwiches, if desired. Makes 8 servings.

Carrot Salad

A popular accompaniment at many Vietnamese meals.

1 **cup water**
3 **tablespoons vinegar**
2 **tablespoons sugar**
   Dash salt
3 **medium carrots, finely shredded**

In a medium mixing bowl combine water, vinegar, sugar, and salt; stir till sugar dissolves. Stir in shredded carrots. Cover and marinate in the refrigerator overnight. Drain carrots before serving. Makes 1½ cups.

Marinated Salmon

8 **fresh *or* frozen salmon *or* other fish steaks (2 to 2½ pounds)**
⅓ **cup sake *or* dry sherry**
⅓ **cup mirin**
¼ **cup soy sauce**
1 **tablespoon cooking oil**
1 **tablespoon lemon juice**
   Lemon wedges *or* lemon slice twists (optional)
   Fresh cilantro *or* parsley (optional)

Thaw fish, if frozen. Rinse and pat dry. For marinade, in a shallow dish combine sake or dry sherry, mirin, soy sauce, oil, and lemon juice. Add fish; cover and marinate in the refrigerator for 4 to 6 hours, turning steaks once.

Drain fish, reserving marinade. Measure thickness of fish. Place fish in a greased shallow baking pan. Bake, uncovered, in a 450° oven till fish flakes easily with a fork. Allow 4 to 6 minutes for each ½ inch of thickness. Brush with some of the reserved marinade after 5 minutes. If desired, garnish with lemon and cilantro or parsley. Makes 8 servings.

Asparagus in Miso

Japanese miso adds a touch of sweetness and a creamy appearance to cold asparagus.

1½ **pounds asparagus *or* two 10-ounce packages frozen cut asparagus**
¼ **cup white miso**
2 **tablespoons sake *or* dry sherry**
1 **tablespoon water**
1 **teaspoon sugar**
1 **tablespoon Toasted Sesame Seed (see recipe, page 10)**

If using fresh asparagus, wash and scrape off scales, if desired. Break off bases at the point where spears snap easily; discard bases. Bias-slice spears into 2-inch pieces.* In a medium saucepan cook asparagus in a small amount of boiling water about 6 minutes or till crisp-tender. (*Or*, cook frozen asparagus according to package directions, omitting salt.) Drain asparagus and set aside.

In a large mixing bowl combine white miso, sake or dry sherry, water, and sugar; mix well. Add asparagus; toss gently. Cover; marinate in the refrigerator for at least 2 hours or overnight. Let asparagus stand at room temperature for 30 minutes before serving; sprinkle with sesame seed. Makes about 3 cups.

See cutting technique, page 27.

Pea Pods with Corn

4 cups fresh pea pods *or* two 6-ounce
    packages frozen pea pods, thawed
1 15-ounce can whole baby sweet corn,
    drained
2 teaspoons cooking oil
2 teaspoons grated gingerroot*
2 green onions, thinly sliced
1 teaspoon sugar
½ teaspoon sesame oil (optional)
¼ teaspoon salt

If using fresh pea pods, remove tips and strings; rinse and drain. Halve baby corn lengthwise, then crosswise; set aside.

(See stir-frying photos, pages 24–25.) Preheat a wok or large skillet over high heat; add cooking oil. Stir-fry gingerroot in hot oil for 15 seconds. Add green onions; stir-fry for 1 minute. Add pea pods; stir-fry for 1 minute. Add corn; sugar; sesame oil, if desired; and salt. Cook and stir about 1 minute or till heated through. Serves 8.

Fruit Platter

4 cups assorted fresh fruit (sliced
    papaya, cubed mango, whole *or* sliced
    strawberries, sliced kiwi fruit, orange
    sections and/*or* pineapple wedges)
1 20-ounce can whole pitted litchis,
    drained
1 15-ounce can whole pitted loquats,
    drained

Arrange fresh fruit, litchis, and loquats on a large serving platter; cover and chill till serving time. Makes 8 servings.

Oriental Menu Planning

Once you've mastered the skills of Oriental cooking, you'll want to share your expertise with friends. But as with any American dinner party, organizing an Oriental party menu requires a little planning and practice. Here are a few ideas to get you started.
● Select foods with eye and taste appeal. All dishes in the meal should complement one another.
● Plan a menu with familiar American foods—ones you are comfortable serving. Then, add an Oriental recipe, such as a soup or a vegetable stir-fry. As you gain confidence, increase the number of Oriental foods on the menu. And don't forget to serve plenty of rice, the mainstay of most Oriental meals.
● As you add more Oriental dishes to the menu, include some that can be made ahead and chilled. Avoid serving more than one or two stir-fries that require last-minute cooking.
● Set the table with rice bowls, tea cups, dinner plates, soup spoons, and chopsticks or forks.
● Place all the food on the table at the same time, including the soup.
● Skip the dessert or offer a selection of fresh fruit. In Oriental countries, sweets are usually reserved for banquets or snacks.

Oriental Ingredients

Need help selecting Oriental ingredients? Then you've turned to the right page. Whether you need lemongrass, fish sauce, or udon, you'll find these next few pages valuable.

Look for these products in the Oriental section at your supermarket, or visit an Oriental grocer. If you can't find an ingredient, use our suggested substitute. Or, if it's a seasoning, simply omit the item from the recipe. Although the flavor will be changed somewhat, you can still enjoy the dish.

Cereal and Bean Products

Bean Threads (4)
Also called cellophane noodles, bean threads are made from ground mung beans. Soften in hot water before using.

Buckwheat Noodles (10)
Known as soba in Japan, these thin dried noodles are made from buckwheat flour. Substitute dried fine egg noodles, if desired.

Egg Noodles, Chinese (1)
Made from wheat flour, water, and egg, Chinese noodles are sold fresh or dried. Substitute American-made fine egg noodles, if desired.

Egg Roll Wrappers (15)
These thin square sheets of noodle dough are called egg roll wrappers or skins. Buy them fresh or frozen.

Fermented Bean Curd (17)
Sometimes called bean curd cheese, fermented bean curd is sold in two forms. The "white" is fermented with or without chili, and the "red" is fermented with rice wine and salt.

Fermented Black Beans (13)
These soybeans are cooked, fermented in a salt brine, then dried. Rinse and finely chop before using.

Hot Bean Paste (7)
A thick reddish sauce with a fiery flavor, hot bean paste combines soybeans, chili peppers, and spices.

Miso (8)
A fermented soybean paste that includes other grains, miso is a Japanese product sold in many colors, textures, and flavors.

Potsticker Wrappers (14)
Made from flour and water, these round dumpling wrappers can be purchased or made at home.

Rice, Long Grain (3)
A staple in most Chinese diets, long grain rice is preferred by most Chinese cooks over the short grain varieties.

Rice Papers (11)
Thin and brittle, dried round rice papers are made from rice flour and used as a wrapper by Vietnamese cooks.

Rice, Short Grain (5)
A favorite of Japanese cooks, short grain rice is slightly sticky when it is cooked.

Rice Sticks (9)
Made from rice flour, rice sticks are also called rice noodles or rice vermicelli. Soften in hot water before using. Substitute cooked fine egg noodles, if desired.

Sweet Bean Sauce (6)
Made from fermented soybeans, sweet bean sauce has a salty sweet flavor. Substitute hoisin sauce, if desired.

Tofu (16)
Soybeans are used to make this custardlike high-protein food. Tofu is also called fresh bean curd or bean cake.

Udon (2)
Also known as white noodles, this thick, broad Japanese pasta is made from wheat flour. Buy it fresh or dried.

Wonton Wrappers (12)
Prepared from noodle dough, these wrappers or skins are sold fresh or frozen. Substitute egg roll wrappers, cut into quarters, if desired.

Fruits and Vegetables

Baby Sweet Corn (10)
Miniature in size, baby corn is 1½ to 2 inches long. Buy it canned.

Bamboo Shoots (17)
These ivory-colored shoots come sliced or cone shaped. Buy the shoots canned.

Bean Sprouts (19)
Grown from mung beans, fresh bean sprouts are white, with tiny caps and a crisp texture. Buy them fresh or canned.

Bok Choy (15)
A Chinese cabbage with white stalks and dark green leaves, bok choy has a sweet flavor.

Chili Peppers (21)
Asian chili peppers are often unavailable in the United States. Substitute serrano or jalapeño peppers. Always handle with gloved hands to protect your skin from the pepper oils.

Chinese Cabbage (11)
Sometimes called Napa or celery cabbage, this elongated cabbage has a mild sweet flavor and pale green wrinkled leaves.

Cilantro (9)
Also called fresh coriander or Chinese parsley, cilantro has a stronger flavor and fragrance than American parsley.

Daikon (8)
This large sweet-tasting Japanese white radish may be long or round. Substitute turnip or American white radish, if desired.

Enoki Mushrooms (20)
Also known as enokitake mushrooms, enoki are prized for their tiny caps, delicate flavor, and crisp texture.

Gingerroot (7)
Gingerroot has a brown skin and a cream-colored flesh, with a pungent flavor.

Kiwi Fruit (6)
Initially known as the Chinese gooseberry, kiwi fruit has a fuzzy brown skin and a tart-sweet green flesh with tiny black seeds. Peel before using.

Lemongrass (12)
Lemon-flavored lemongrass resembles a fibrous green onion. Buy it fresh or dried. Substitute lemon peel, if desired.

11
15
18
12
19
16
20
13
21
14
17
22

Litchi (3)
Also spelled lychee, this sweet juicy white fruit has a hard red shell. Litchis are most often sold canned.

Loquat (4)
Orange-colored fruit with a slightly tart flavor, loquats are available canned or dried.

Mango (2)
Ripe mangoes vary in color from green to yellow to red. They taste similar to apricots and have juicy flesh.

Oriental Chrysanthemum Leaves (18)
These fresh greens are called shungiku in Japan. *Do not* confuse them with the toxic common flowering plant. Discard the roots and flowering buds before using.

Papaya (5)
When ripe, this pear-shape fruit has yellowish skin and buttery-tasting golden flesh. Edible peppery black seeds fill the center cavity.

Pea Pods (16)
Also known as sugar peas or snowpeas, pea pods conceal flat tiny peas. They have a sweet flavor and crisp, firm texture. Buy them fresh or frozen.

Pickled Ginger (14)
Preserved in vinegar, pickled ginger may be red, pink, or light yellow. Eat with sushi.

Straw Mushrooms (22)
Cultivated on rice straw, these dark mushrooms have a "meaty" texture. Buy them canned or dried. Substitute another variety of canned mushrooms, if desired.

Taro Root (1)
A potatolike vegetable, taro root has dark, hairy skin and light-colored flesh. Peel before using. Substitute white potato, if desired.

Water Chestnuts (13)
About the size of walnuts, water chestnuts are a root vegetable with a crisp white flesh. Buy them canned or fresh. Canned water chestnuts are peeled. If you buy them fresh, peel before using.

Special Helps

Seasonings and Dried Products

Black Sesame Seed (14)
Sesame seed may be black or white. It is often toasted to enhance the flavor.

Bonita Flakes (7)
Known as katsuo bushi in Japan, bonita flakes are shaved from dried bonita (a member of the mackerel family). Use to make dashi.

Chinese Sausage (1)
This highly flavored wind-dried sausage is made with pork or liver. Cook before eating. Substitute smoked sausage or dried salami, if desired.

Dashi-No-Moto (8)
This stock base is sold in powdered form. Mix with water and use as an instant substitute for dashi, if desired.

Dried Cloud Ears (13)
Smaller in size and more delicate in flavor than wood ears, these edible fungi absorb flavors from other foods and add a crunchy texture. Soak cloud ears in hot water, then rinse and remove the tough stems before using.

Dried Lily Buds (12)
Sold as tiger-lily buds or golden needles, these dried buds add texture and a delicate flavor to Oriental dishes. Soak in hot water before using.

Dried Mushrooms (18)
Also known as dried black mushrooms or winter mushrooms, these crinkly edible tree fungi add a chewy texture and a smoky flavor to Oriental dishes. The Japanese variety is called shiitaki. Soak mushrooms in hot water, then rinse and remove the tough stems before using.

Dried Red Chili Peppers (3)
Hot and fiery, dried chili peppers are popular in many Oriental cuisines. To reduce hotness, remove the seeds before using. Handle with gloved hands to protect your skin from the pepper oils.

Dried Shrimp (10)
Shelled, salted, and sun-dried, these tiny shrimp have a sharp flavor and aroma. The color may vary. Soak in hot water before using.

11 12 13 14 15 16 17 18 10

Dried Tangerine Peel (16)

Dark brown and brittle, tangerine peel is sun-dried to produce a seasoning with a pungent flavor. Substitute your own home-dried peel (see tip, page 11), if desired.

Dried Wood Ears (17)

Also sold as tree ears, these large edible mushrooms are coarser in texture than cloud ears. Soak in hot water, then remove the tough stems before using.

Five-Spice Powder (6)

This fragrant mix of spices includes cinnamon, star anise, fennel, Szechwan peppers, and cloves. Other spices may be added. Substitute your own homemade blend (see tip, page 11), if desired.

Ground Laos (4)

Laos is the Indonesian name for galangal root, which is a member of the ginger family. More aromatic and delicate in flavor than ginger, laos is sold dried or ground.

Kelp (9)

Called konbu in Japanese, kelp comes from the sea and is used to make dashi. The white powder found on the dried sheets adds a sweet flavor to the stock.

Nori Seaweed (11)

A common seaweed eaten in Japan, nori is used as a sushi wrap. Toast to enhance the flavor before using.

Star Anise (15)

This star-shape spice has a licoricelike flavor and aroma. Substitute 1 teaspoon ground aniseed for one star anise, if desired.

Wasabi Powder (5)

Known as Japanese horseradish, wasabi is unrelated to our horseradish but similar in flavor. Buy the light green powder and mix with water to form a paste. Wasabi is also sold as a paste.

Whole Szechwan Peppers (2)

Reddish brown in color, these berries produce a slight numbing effect on the tongue. Substitute whole black peppers, if desired.

Sauces and Flavorings

Chili Oil (17)
Flavored with chili peppers, chili oil adds hotness to Oriental dishes. Substitute your own homemade oil (see tip, page 11), if desired.

Chili Paste (1)
A fiery condiment, chili paste varies according to the country of origin. When ground soybeans are added, it is called hot bean paste.

Chili Sauce (16)
This tangy, reddish sauce is made with chili peppers, vinegar, and spices. The ingredients and hotness vary, depending upon the country of origin.

Chinese Black Vinegar (9)
Made from rice, black vinegar is commonly used as a dipping sauce and in the preparation of many seafood dishes. Other common types of rice vinegar are white (clear) and red.

Chinese Soy Sauce (5)
Made from fermented soybeans, Chinese soy sauce is sold as light (thin), dark (sweetened with caramel), and black (flavored with molasses) soy sauce.

Fish Sauce (12)
A thin, salty brown liquid made from salted fish, fish sauce is an indispensable seasoning in Southeast Asia and southern China.

Hoisin Sauce (4)
Thick and rich flavored, hoisin sauce is made from soybeans, sugar, garlic, flour, vinegar, and spices.

Japanese Soy Sauce (3)
Made from fermented soybeans, soy sauce is called shoyu in Japan. It is available in two different types: medium-dark and light.

Mirin (11)
A sweet, syrupy Japanese rice wine, mirin is used in glazes and dipping sauces. Because of its low alcohol content, you'll find it in supermarkets or Oriental food shops, rather than in liquor stores. Substitute dry sherry, if desired.

Oyster Sauce (14)
A thick brown sauce made from oysters, this sauce is sometimes used by Chinese cooks instead of soy sauce for flavoring food.

Plum Sauce (18)
A thick fruity dipping sauce, plum sauce has a sweet-tart flavor. It is made with plums and/or apricots, chili peppers, vinegar, sugar, and spices. Substitute your own homemade sauce (see tip, page 11), if desired.

Rice Vinegar (10)
Rice vinegar has a mild, slightly sweet flavor. Chinese rice vinegar is stronger in flavor than Japanese rice vinegar. Substitute white or cider vinegar, if desired.

Rice Wine (8)
Made from fermented rice, rice wine is used as a beverage and for cooking. When it is labeled cooking rice wine, it contains salt and should only be used for cooking. Substitute dry sherry, if desired.

Sake (6)
A flat, colorless Japanese beverage, sake is classified as a beer because of its brewing process. Sake has a high alcohol content and is often served warm for sipping.

Sesame Oil (15)
Thick and aromatic, Chinese sesame oil is made from toasted sesame seed and is golden brown. Because of its strong flavor, it is usually used for flavoring, not for general cooking. Other types of sesame oil are lighter in color and milder in flavor.

Sesame Paste (19)
Made from ground toasted seed, this thick aromatic paste has a nutty flavor similar to peanut buttter. Substitute your own homemade paste (see tip, page 11), if desired.

Shrimp Paste (7)
Available in many forms, shrimp paste is made from fermented shrimp. It has a strong flavor and aroma. Dilute with water before using. Substitute anchovy paste, if desired.

Sweet Soy Sauce (2)
A thick heavy sauce, sweet soy is flavored with molasses. Substitute your own homemade sauce (see tip, page 11), if desired.

Tamarind Paste (13)
Made from the fruit of the tamarind tree, tamarind paste adds a tart flavor to food.

Nutrition Analysis Chart

Use these analyses to compare nutritional values of different recipes. This information was calculated using Agriculture Handbook Number 8, published by the United States Department of Agriculture, as the primary source.

In compiling the nutrition analyses, we made the following assumptions:
- For all of the main-dish meat recipes, the nutrition analyses were calculated using weights or measures for cooked meat.

- Garnishes and optional ingredients were not included in the nutrition analyses.
- If a marinade was brushed over a food during cooking, the analysis includes all of the marinade.
- When two ingredient options appear in a recipe, calculations were made using the first one.
- For ingredients of variable weight (such as "2½- to 3-pound broiler-fryer chicken") or for recipes with a serving range ("Makes 4 to 6 servings"), calculations were made using the first figure.

	Per Serving						Percent U.S. RDA Per Serving							
	Calories	Protein (g)	Carbohydrate (g)	Fat (g)	Sodium (mg)	Potassium (mg)	Protein	Vitamin A	Vitamin C	Thiamine	Riboflavin	Niacin	Calcium	Iron
Appetizers														
Chinese Buns (p. 101)	140	7	20	4	110	150	10	0	0	20	10	10	2	6
Chinese Egg Rolls (p. 99)	120	8	15	3	105	270	10	80	6	8	10	20	0	4
Chinese Roast Pork (p. 10)	60	11	1	2	95	200	15	0	0	25	8	8	0	2
Deep-Fried Phoenix-Tailed Shrimp (p. 84)	110	11	10	3	250	130	15	0	0	2	2	10	6	6
Deep-Fried Wontons (p. 89)	40	2	5	2	55	30	2	0	0	4	0	2	0	0
Four-Flavored Dumplings (p. 96)	50	3	9	1	80	65	4	6	0	6	4	4	0	2
Grilled Scallops (p. 67)	80	12	6	0	770	340	20	0	0	4	2	6	2	8
Makizushi (p. 60)	40	2	5	1	190	40	2	8	0	2	2	0	0	2
Moo Shu Pork with Mandarin Pancakes (p. 108)	210	9	16	12	290	210	15	40	4	25	10	10	2	8
Nigirizushi (p. 61)	25	2	4	0	35	25	2	0	0	0	0	·2	0	0
Oven-Roasted Spareribs (p. 8)	50	6	4	1	85	115	8	0	0	10	4	4	0	2
Potstickers (p. 100)	60	2	7	2	60	40	4	0	0	8	2	4	0	2
Skewered Pork (p. 100)	60	8	1	3	85	140	10	0	0	30	4	8	0	0
Vietnamese Spring Rolls (p. 92)	40	2	3	2	25	35	2	10	0	2	0	2	0	0
Fillings														
Date Filling (p. 89)	60	1	12	2	0	90	0	0	0	0	0	0	0	0
Peanut Butter Filling (p. 89)	100	4	6	7	65	110	6	0	0	0	0	8	0	2
Pork and Shrimp Filling (p. 88)	25	3	1	1	60	45	4	0	0	2	0	2	0	0
Pork Filling (p. 101)	25	2	1	1	25	55	2	0	0	4	2	2	0	0
Sweet Bean-Date Filling (p. 101)	50	1	6	2	0	80	0	0	0	0	0	0	0	0

	Per Serving						Percent U.S. RDA Per Serving							
	Calories	Protein (g)	Carbohydrate (g)	Fat (g)	Sodium (mg)	Potassium (mg)	Protein	Vitamin A	Vitamin C	Thiamine	Riboflavin	Niacin	Calcium	Iron
Main Dishes														
Beef and Cabbage Rolls (p. 72)	120	7	2	9	60	135	10	0	7	2	4	6	0	6
Beef and Peppers in Black Bean Sauce (p. 30)	210	24	8	8	1100	430	35	4	60	8	15	25	2	20
Beef and Tomatoes with Fried Noodles (p. 46)	310	21	34	9	480	380	30	10	37	25	15	30	2	20
Cantonese Firepot (p. 53)	310	37	21	8	2080	970	60	70	34	20	25	60	15	30
Cantonese Lemon Chicken (p. 84)	360	31	24	15	540	390	45	4	15	8	10	70	4	10
Chicken and Vegetable One-Pot (p. 50)	230	32	13	5	1010	490	50	60	11	8	15	70	8	20
Chicken in Soy Sauce (p. 10)	170	30	1	5	250	270	45	0	4	4	6	70	0	6
Crispy Szechwan Duck (p. 104)	290	24	12	16	930	430	35	2	9	30	35	35	4	25
Egg Dumplings with Pork (p. 56)	220	15	8	14	790	610	25	100	35	15	20	10	10	20
Fried Rice with Chicken (p. 41)	390	24	41	14	210	270	35	8	6	20	8	40	10	20
Fried Rice with Sausage and Crab (p. 41)	460	18	39	25	820	210	25	10	2	30	10	15	6	15
Indonesian Chicken Saté (p. 66)	130	20	1	4	310	190	30	0	0	2	6	40	0	4
Kung Pao Chicken (p. 32)	340	32	19	14	690	420	50	4	4	10	10	70	2	10
Malaysian Fish with Hot Chili Sauce (p. 70)	330	31	10	17	220	710	45	90	20	20	10	25	6	8
Marinated Salmon (p. 112)	220	24	2	11	570	430	35	2	0	10	8	0	0	6
Mongolian Firepot (p. 52)	400	29	23	21	1570	730	45	30	24	20	25	50	20	30
Nasi Goreng (p. 40)	410	26	43	15	750	540	40	4	6	50	15	25	6	20
Peking Lamb with Green Onions (p. 35)	210	24	4	9	470	330	35	0	4	8	10	25	0	10
Pork with Fish Flavor (p. 33)	260	22	12	13	1070	450	35	4	4	30	15	25	2	8
Red-Cooked Beef (p. 111)	210	24	13	7	2120	380	35	0	3	4	10	25	2	20
Red-Cooked Chicken (p. 14)	180	30	4	3	760	300	45	0	0	4	6	70	2	8
Red-Cooked Cornish Game Hens (p. 14)	320	40	20	5	4270	710	60	0	10	10	20	80	6	25
Red-Cooked Squabs (p. 14)	270	31	5	13	1120	490	50	2	0	30	30	60	2	45
Roast Pork with Crispy Noodles (p. 46)	360	29	35	10	400	640	45	4	4	70	30	35	2	15
Shrimp Saté (p. 67)	160	17	5	9	530	280	25	4	11	2	2	20	6	8
Steamed Chicken and Vegetables (p. 73)	170	28	6	3	70	500	40	15	18	8	8	60	2	8
Steamed Eggs with Mushrooms (p. 75)	240	16	17	13	230	300	25	20	23	25	20	8	6	10
Stir-Fried Chicken with Noodle Cake (p. 44)	340	26	37	9	750	510	40	160	50	30	20	60	8	15
Sweet and Sour Pork (p. 85)	490	23	42	25	700	620	35	110	110	40	20	25	4	20
Szechwan-Style Pork and Cabbage (p. 34)	180	15	6	11	340	500	25	50	80	30	10	15	10	8
Tempura (p. 82)	310	15	25	15	660	350	25	60	25	10	10	20	6	15
Thai Chicken Saté (p. 64)	250	28	4	14	70	360	40	0	4	4	6	60	2	10
Sauces														
Chili Oil Dipping Sauce (p. 100)	10	1	1	0	410	35	0	0	0	0	0	0	0	0
Hot Mustard Sauce (p. 10)	30	1	2	2	0	30	0	0	0	0	0	0	2	2
Nuoc Cham (p. 40)	20	0	5	0	105	25	0	4	10	0	0	0	0	0
Peanut Dipping Sauce (p. 64)	80	3	2	7	115	85	4	0	0	0	0	6	0	0

	Per Serving						Percent U.S. RDA Per Serving								
	Calories	Protein (g)	Carbohydrate (g)	Fat (g)	Sodium (mg)	Potassium (mg)	Protein	Vitamin A	Vitamin C	Thiamine	Riboflavin	Niacin	Calcium	Iron
Sauces (continued)														
Sesame Paste Dip (p. 52)	50	1	2	4	180	45	2	0	0	0	0	2	4	6
Soy-Vinegar Sauce (p. 53)	8	1	1	0	550	45	0	0	0	0	0	0	0	0
Sweet and Sour Sauce (p. 99)	20	0	5	0	130	45	0	0	8	0	0	0	0	0
Sweet Soy Dipping Sauce (p. 72)	4	0	1	0	280	250	0	0	2	0	0	0	0	0
Tempura Dipping Sauce (p. 82)	6	0	1	0	150	10	0	0	0	0	0	0	0	0
Side Dishes														
Asparagus in Miso (p. 112)	35	2	4	1	0	210	2	10	35	6	4	4	0	2
Bean Sprouts with Carrots (p. 26)	90	3	11	4	190	280	4	280	15	6	6	4	2	4
Broccoli in Oyster Sauce (p. 24)	90	4	13	4	85	420	6	25	100	4	10	8	4	4
Carrot Salad (p. 112)	25	0	6	0	25	95	0	150	4	0	0	0	0	0
Cucumber Salad (p. 66)	40	0	10	0	70	105	0	4	9	0	0	0	0	0
Kimchi (p. 111)	30	2	5	1	65	280	2	50	52	2	4	2	10	4
Pea Pods with Corn (p. 113)	35	2	5	1	135	90	2	2	25	4	2	0	2	2
Szechwan Stir-Fried Cabbage (p. 26)	70	3	7	4	590	360	4	90	80	2	6	4	10	8
Yangchow Fried Rice (p. 38)	250	14	31	8	660	260	20	4	8	25	6	15	4	15
Soups														
Chicken and Vegetable Soup (p. 21)	140	17	12	3	200	490	25	120	15	6	6	30	8	10
Hot and Sour Shrimp Soup (p. 20)	110	14	2	5	810	320	20	8	20	0	4	25	4	6
Korean Beef Soup (p. 20)	140	13	6	7	810	420	20	100	8	6	10	20	2	10
Spicy Chicken Soup (p. 18)	260	22	19	10	810	570	35	0	8	8	10	50	4	10
Wonton Soup (p. 88)	140	11	16	3	880	450	15	50	14	15	10	20	6	10
Miscellaneous														
Chinese Boiled Rice (p. 38)	110	2	25	0	90	30	2	0	0	8	0	4	0	4
Dashi (p. 20)	0	0	0	0	0	0	0	0	0	0	0	0	0	0
Fruit Platter (p. 113)	70	1	19	0	0	280	0	30	110	2	4	2	0	2
Lotus Leaf Buns (p. 74)	100	2	15	3	60	50	2	0	0	8	6	6	0	4
Pan-Fried Noodle Cake (p. 44)	170	5	27	4	0	50	6	0	0	20	8	10	0	6
Steamed Jelly Roll (p. 75)	130	2	27	2	35	40	2	0	0	2	4	0	0	2
Steamed Silver-Thread Buns (p. 78)	160	3	26	5	95	40	4	2	0	10	8	8	0	8

A–B

Appetizers
  Chinese Buns, 101
  Chinese Egg Rolls, 99
  Chinese Roast Pork, 10
  Deep-Fried Phoenix-Tailed
    Shrimp, 84
  Deep-Fried Wontons, 89
  Four-Flavored Dumplings, 96
  Grilled Scallops, 67
  Makizushi, 6
  Nigirizushi, 61
  Oriental Cold Plate, 111
  Oven-Roasted Spareribs, 8
  Potstickers, 100
  Skewered Pork, 100
  Vietnamese Spring Rolls, 92
Asparagus in Miso, 112
Barbecuing
  Arranging hot coals, 65
  Grilled Scallops, 67
  Indonesian Chicken Saté, 66
  Shrimp Saté, 67
  Thai Chicken Saté, 64
Bean Sprouts with Carrots, 26
Beef
  Beef and Cabbage Rolls, 72
  Beef and Peppers in Black
    Bean Sauce, 30
  Beef and Tomatoes with Fried
    Noodles, 46
  Cantonese Firepot, 53
  Korean Beef Soup, 20
  Nasi Goreng, 40
  Red-Cooked Beef, 111
Bias-slicing meat, 35
Bias-slicing vegetables, 27
Broccoli in Oyster Sauce, 24

Buns
  Chinese Buns, 101
  Lotus Leaf Buns, 74
  Steamed Silver-Thread
    Buns, 78

C

Cantonese Firepot, 53
Cantonese Lemon Chicken, 84
Carrot Flowers, 14
Carrot Salad, 112
Chicken
  Cantonese Firepot, 53
  Cantonese Lemon
    Chicken, 84
  Chicken and Vegetable
    One-Pot, 50
  Chicken and Vegetable
    Soup, 21
  Chicken in Soy Sauce, 10
  Chinese Egg Rolls, 99
  Cubing chicken, 35
  Fried Rice with Chicken, 41
  Indonesian Chicken Saté, 66
  Kung Pao Chicken, 32
  Red-Cooked Chicken, 14
  Spicy Chicken Soup, 18
  Steamed Chicken and
    Vegetables, 73
  Stir-Fried Chicken with Noodle
    Cake, 44
  Thai Chicken Saté, 64
Chili Oil, 11
Chili Oil Dipping Sauce, 100
Chili Pepper Flower, 30

Chinese Boiled Rice, 38
Chinese Buns, 101
Chinese Egg Rolls, 99
Chinese Roast Pork, 10
Coconut Milk, 64
Cornish Game Hens,
  Red-Cooked, 14
Crab
  Fried Rice with Sausage and
    Crab, 41
  Vietnamese Spring Rolls, 92
Crispy Szechwan Duck, 104
Cucumber Salad, 66
Cucumber Sticks, 9

D–G

Dashi, 20
Date Filling, 89
Deep-Fried Phoenix-Tailed
  Shrimp, 84
Deep-Fried Wontons, 89
Desserts
  Fruit Platter, 113
  Steamed Jelly Roll, 75
Dip, Sesame Paste, 52
Dried Tangerine Peel, 11
Duck, Crispy Szechwan, 104
Dumpling Dough, 96
Dumplings
  Egg Dumplings with Pork, 56
  Four-Flavored Dumplings, 96
  Potstickers, 100
Egg Dumplings with Pork, 56
Egg Rolls, Chinese, 99
Egg sheet, 39
Eggs with Mushrooms,
  Steamed, 75

Fillings
  Date Filling, 89
  Peanut Butter Filling, 89
  Pork and Shrimp Filling, 88
  Pork Filling, 101
  Sweet Bean-Date Filling, 101
Fish with Hot Chili Sauce,
  Malaysian, 70
Five-Spice Powder, 11
Four-Flavored Dumplings, 96
Fried Onion Flakes, 19
Fried Rice
  Fried Rice with Chicken, 41
  Fried Rice with Sausage and
    Crab, 41
  Nasi Goreng, 40
  Yangchow Fried Rice, 38
Fruit Platter, 113
Garnishes
  Carrot Flowers, 14
  Chili Pepper Flower, 30
  Cucumber Sticks, 9
  Fried Onion Flakes, 19
  Green Onion Brushes, 71
  Toasted Sesame Seed, 10
Grating gingerroot, 27
Green Onion Brushes, 71
Grilled Scallops, 67

H–O

Hot and Sour Shrimp Soup, 20
Hot Mustard Sauce, 10
Indonesia
  Beef and Cabbage Rolls, 72
  Chicken in Soy Sauce, 10
  Cucumber Salad, 66
  Indonesian Chicken Saté, 66
  Nasi Goreng, 40

Indonesia *(continued)*
  Peanut Dipping Sauce, 64
  Spicy Chicken Soup, 18
  Sweet Soy Dipping Sauce, 72
Japan
  Asparagus in Miso, 112
  Chicken and Vegetable
    One-Pot, 50
  Chicken and Vegetable
    Soup, 21
  Dashi, 20
  Grilled Scallops, 67
  Makizushi, 60
  Marinated Salmon, 112
  Nigirizushi, 61
  Tempura, 82
  Tempura Dipping Sauce, 82
Jelly Roll, Steamed, 75
Julienne-cutting vegetables, 27
Kimchi, 111
Korea
  Kimchi, 111
  Korean Beef Soup, 20
Kung Pao Chicken, 32
Lamb
  Lamb with Green Onions,
    Peking, 35
  Mongolian Firepot, 52
Lotus Leaf Buns, 74
Makizushi, 60
Malaysia
  Malaysian Fish with Hot Chili
    Sauce, 70
  Nasi Goreng, 40
  Shrimp Saté, 67
  Spicy Chicken Soup, 18
Mandarin Pancakes, 108
Marinated Salmon, 112

Marinating meat, 8
Microwave
  Attention, Microwave
    Owners!, 73
  Steamed Chicken and
    Vegetables, 73
  Sweet and Sour Sauce, 99
Mincing garlic, 27
Mongolian Firepot, 52
Moo Shu Pork with Mandarin
  Pancakes, 108
Mustard Sauce, Hot, 10
Nasi Goreng, 40
Nigirizushi, 61
Noodles
  Beef and Tomatoes with Fried
    Noodles, 46
  Cantonese Firepot, 53
  Chicken and Vegetable
    One-Pot, 50
  Mongolian Firepot, 52
  Noodle Cake, Pan-Fried, 44
  Roast Pork with Crispy
    Noodles, 46
  Stir-Fried Chicken with Noodle
    Cake, 44
Nuoc Cham, 40
Omelet Roll, 60
Onion Flakes, Fried, 19
Oriental Cold Plate, 111
Oven-Roasted Spareribs, 8
Oyster Sauce, Broccoli in, 24

P–R

Pancakes, Mandarin, 108
Pan-Fried Noodle Cake, 44
Peanut Butter Filling, 89
Peanut Dipping Sauce, 64
Pea Pods with Corn, 113

Peking Lamb with Green
   Onions, 35
Pepper-Salt, Szechwan, 84
Plum Sauce, 11
Pork
   Chinese Roast Pork, 10
   Egg Dumplings with Pork, 56
   Moo Shu Pork with Mandarin
      Pancakes, 108
   Nasi Goreng, 40
   Oven-Roasted Spareribs, 8
   Pork and Shrimp Filling, 88
   Pork Filling, 101
   Pork with Fish Flavor, 33
   Potstickers, 100
   Roast Pork with Crispy
      Noodles, 46
   Skewered Pork, 100
   Steamed Eggs with
      Mushrooms, 75
   Sweet and Sour Pork, 85
   Szechwan-Style Pork and
      Cabbage, 34
   Vietnamese Spring Rolls, 92
   Yangchow Fried Rice, 38
Potstickers, 100
Red-Cooking
   Red-Cooked Beef, 111
   Red-Cooked Chicken, 14
   Red-Cooked Cornish Game
      Hens, 14
   Red-Cooked Squabs, 14
Rice
   Chinese Boiled Rice, 38
   Cooking rice, 39
   Fried Rice with Chicken, 41
   Fried Rice with Sausage and
      Crab, 41
   Nasi Goreng, 40
   Vinegared Rice, 60

Rice *(continued)*
   Washing rice, 39
   Yangchow Fried Rice, 38
Rice sticks, cutting, 18
Roasting
   Chicken in Soy Sauce, 10
   Chinese Roast Pork, 10
   Oven-Roasted Spareribs, 8
Roast Pork with Crispy
   Noodles, 46
Roll-cutting vegetables, 27

S

Salad, Carrot, 112
Salad, Cucumber, 66
Salmon, Marinated, 112
Satés
   Indonesian Chicken Saté, 66
   Shrimp Saté, 67
   Skewered Pork, 100
   Thai Chicken Saté, 64
Sauces
   Chili Oil Dipping Sauce, 100
   Hot Mustard Sauce, 10
   Nuoc Cham, 40
   Peanut Dipping Sauce, 64
   Plum Sauce, 11
   Sesame Paste Dip, 52
   Soy-Vinegar Sauce, 53
   Sweet and Sour Sauce, 99
   Sweet Soy Dipping Sauce, 72
   Sweet Soy Sauce, 11
   Tempura Dipping Sauce, 82
Sausage and Crab, Fried Rice
   with, 41

Scallops
   Cantonese Firepot, 53
   Grilled Scallops, 67
   Tempura, 82
Sesame Paste, 11
Sesame Paste Dip, 52
Sesame Seed, Toasted, 10
Shredding meat, 35
Shrimp
   Cantonese Firepot, 53
   Deep-Fried Phoenix-Tailed
      Shrimp, 84
   Hot and Sour Shrimp
      Soup, 20
   Nasi Goreng, 40
   Pork and Shrimp Filling, 88
   Shrimp Saté, 67
   Tempura, 82
   Yangchow Fried Rice, 38
Silver-Thread Buns,
   Steamed, 78
Skewered Pork, 100
Slivering green onions, 27
Soups
   Chicken and Vegetable
      Soup, 21
   Hot and Sour Shrimp
      Soup, 20
   Korean Beef Soup, 20
   Spicy Chicken Soup, 18
   Wonton Soup, 88
Soy-Vinegar Sauce, 53
Spice bag, 14
Spicy Chicken Soup, 18
Spring Rolls, Vietnamese, 92
Squabs, Red-Cooked, 14
Steaming
   Beef and Cabbage Rolls, 72
   Chinese Buns, 101
   Four-Flavored Dumplings, 96

Steaming *(continued)*
  Lotus Leaf Buns, 74
  Malaysian Fish with Hot Chili
    Sauce, 70
  Steamed Chicken and
    Vegetables, 73
  Steamed Eggs with
    Mushrooms, 75
  Steamed Jelly Roll, 75
  Steamed Silver-Thread
    Buns, 78
Stir-Frying
  Bean Sprouts with
    Carrots, 26
  Beef and Peppers in Black
    Bean Sauce, 30
  Beef and Tomatoes with Fried
    Noodles, 46
  Broccoli in Oyster Sauce, 24
  Cantonese Lemon
    Chicken, 84
  Kung Pao Chicken, 32
  Moo Shu Pork with Mandarin
    Pancakes, 108
  Pea Pods with Corn, 113
  Peking Lamb with Green
    Onions, 35
  Pork with Fish Flavor, 33
  Roast Pork with Crispy
    Noodles, 46
  Stir-Fried Chicken with Noodle
    Cake, 44
  Stir-frying
    techniques, 24–25, 31
  Sweet and Sour Pork, 85
  Szechwan Stir-Fried
    Cabbage, 26
  Szechwan-Style Pork and
    Cabbage, 34
Straining stock, 15

Sushi
  Makizushi, 60
  Nigirizushi, 61
  Vinegared Rice, 60
Sweet and Sour Pork, 85
Sweet and Sour Sauce, 99
Sweet Bean-Date Filling, 101
Sweet Soy Dipping Sauce, 72
Sweet Soy Sauce, 11
Szechwan Pepper-Salt, 84
Szechwan Stir-Fried
  Cabbage, 26
Szechwan-Style Pork and
  Cabbage, 34

T–Z

Tangerine Peel, Dried, 11
Tempura, 82
Tempura Dipping Sauce, 82
Thailand
  Cucumber Salad, 66
  Fried Rice with Chicken, 41
  Hot and Sour Soup, 20
  Peanut Dipping Sauce, 64
  Thai Chicken Saté, 64
Toasted Sesame Seed, 10
Vegetables
  Asparagus in Miso, 112
  Bean Sprouts with
    Carrots, 26
  Bias slicing, 27
  Broccoli in Oyster Sauce, 24
  Grating, 27
  Julienne cutting, 27
  Kimchi, 111
  Mincing, 27
  Pea Pods with Corn, 113
  Roll cutting, 27
  Slivering, 27

Vegetables *(continued)*
  Steamed Chicken and
    Vegetables, 73
  Szechwan Stir-Fried
    Cabbage, 26
  Tempura, 82
Vietnam
  Carrot Salad, 112
  Fried Rice with Sausage and
    Crab, 41
  Nuoc Cham, 41
  Steamed Eggs with
    Mushrooms, 75
  Vietnamese Spring Rolls, 92
Vinegared Rice, 60
Wontons, Deep-Fried, 89
Wonton Soup, 88
Yangchow Fried Rice, 38

Tips

Attention, Microwave
  Owners!, 73
Boning Chicken Breasts, 34
Cleaning Shrimp, 21
Cuisines at a Glance, 47
Cutting Meat and Poultry, 35
Cutting Vegetables, 27
Firepot Safety, 53
Homemade Ingredients, 11
Oriental Menu Planning, 113
Oriental-Style Carving, 105
Successful Steaming, 74
Using Chopsticks, 50